Ethics and Economic Theory

Ethics and Economic Theory

Ideas – Models – Dilemmas

Kurt W. Rothschild

Professor Emeritus of Economics
University of Linz, Austria

Edward Elgar

Published by
Edward Elgar Publishing Limited
Gower House
Croft Road
Aldershot
Hants GU11 3HR
UK

Edward Elgar Publishing Company
Old Post Road
Brookfield
Vermont 05036
US

Reprinted 1995

A CIP catalogue record for this book is available from the British Library

ISBN 1 85278 675 2

Printed in Great Britain by Antony Rowe Ltd, Chippenham, Witlshire

Contents

Figures

Preface

Few people will deny that there are some connections between ethics and economics and that there should be some relationships between the two. Not only are such norms as 'Thou shalt not steal' of obvious relevance in everyday economic life, there is also a host of other relations like those between trading partners, between employers and employees etc. which have ethical and moral connotations. 'Ethics in economic life', 'Business ethics' and similar themes are therefore frequently taken up and have obtained a place in university curricula.

These questions and perspectives are not the subject of this book. As its title suggests, it is concerned exclusively with the relationships between economic *science*, economic theories and ethics (in a very wide sense). In this connection it is not so obvious that the two disciplines have some common ground. After all, the task of economic science is to analyse and to 'explain' the economic process, but not necessarily to pass judgements whether these processes are 'good' or 'bad' or to prescribe 'proper' actions for the economic agents. Just as natural scientists deal with the laws of nature, economic theorists could restrict themselves to a study of the 'laws' of economics without ever touching ethical questions. It turns out, however, that such a clear-cut division does not exist. Quite apart from the fact that in all social and human sciences an entry of ethically relevant factors is practically unavoidable, we find that economic theories contain explicitly or implicitly many aspects which have ethical implications. And this quite irrespective of avowed declarations about a desired adherence to 'scientific', 'objective', 'pure' standards. The ethical aspects often creep in quite unintended and may not be easily recognizable as such.

This problem of ethical elements in economic theories and models forms the subject of this book. It is not claimed that this is a completely new undertaking – all the questions which will be treated have been touched by others before – nor can a complete and systematic treatment of all questions be expected since this is probably an impossible task anyway. The aim is the more modest attempt to offer an overview of the wide spectre of economic-ethical-theoretical interdependencies by presenting some relevant problem areas in a relatively simple fashion.

The book is meant for students of economics and other persons interested in economic theory. Some elementary knowledge of economic theory is assumed, while ethical theory is only occasionally touched upon when this is necessary in a certain connection. In a more comprehensive interdisciplinary study more room would have to be given to moral philosophy and ethical science. It would then also be necessary to show in greater detail how ethics can profit from economic theory. The theory of choice can throw light on the problem of ethical dilemmas, and knowledge of economic theory would help to prevent ethical demands from turning utopian. These questions will not be treated. The book could nevertheless also be of interest to students of ethics aiming at a better basis for discussions with economists and the avoidance of misunderstandings.

This book has benefited from a series of discussions on ethics and economics at the *Evangelische Akademie* in Tutzing and the *Evangelische Akademie* in Loccum (both in Germany). I am grateful to many of the participants for interesting ideas and doubts. The same applies to the students at the University of Graz (Austria) where I gave a course on this subject in 1991. Particular thanks are due to Edward Elgar for the interest he has shown and to Julie Leppard for her extensive and efficient editorial help. Monika Mayer-Exner produced a neat typescript in record time. Since it has become a routine matter to thank one's wife for her patience and forbearance I shall refrain from doing so.

1. On Ethics

In the preface it was already stressed that this book deals with problems and relations between ethics and economic theory mainly from the perspective of the latter. This means that we can content ourselves with a fairly wide definition of ethics without having to go into details about various special approaches and inner-ethical disputes. It will nonetheless be quite useful to start off with some general remarks on ethics which can serve as a background to our later considerations. These remarks can cover only a limited number of points, and preference will be given to questions which are relevant to our discussion. This means that utilitarianism in particular will receive special attention because it played a major role in the formative years of modern economic theory in the 18th and 19th centuries and has remained an important influence until today.

It is good practice to start off with a definition of the terms under discussion. In the case of 'ethics' this is not easy: rigid definitions tend to be too narrow for our purpose; wider definitions are usually too vague. Thus we are told in the *International Encyclopedia of Social Sciences* that 'ethics is concerned with standards of conduct among people in social groups.'[1] This is certainly a very wide definition which includes norms and conventions which we would hardly call 'ethical norms'.[2] Other definitions try to narrow down this very general statement by stipulating additional characteristics such as a special importance for human relations, the existence of social (though not necessarily legal) sanctions, etc. But no matter which definition one chooses, a residue of fuzziness remains regarding the distinctions between 'ethics' and 'morals'. Frequently the adjective 'ethical' is reserved for more serious aspects of human relations which are connected with strong emotions and social sanctions, while questions of 'moral behaviour' are regarded as less weighty. But the frontiers are not easily drawn and in what follows we shall sometimes use the terms 'ethics' and 'morals' synonymously.[3]

Dealing with ethics and economics we are entering an interdisciplinary discussion concerning two separate disciplines. The first question one might ask is: How far are these two disciplines commensurable? Economics, as we know it, regards itself predominantly as a 'positive' science making statements about things as they are. Yet it is a fact that economic literature contains quite a lot of 'normative' elements; that is, open or implicit statements as to how things 'ought' to be.

What is the position of ethics in this respect? In the case of ethics the differentiation between positive and normative aspects is less problematic than in economics because ethics does not pretend to be exclusively a positive science. It therefore does not suffer from inhibitions to present its normative side quite openly. It is important to distinguish between three different strands in the study of ethics:

1. the study of the origin and the dynamics of ethical norms;
2. construction of philosophical systems as a basis for ethical judgements, and
3. moral codes.

As far as (1) is concerned, we are dealing with a positive branch of ethical studies which tries to explain actual ethical norms and behaviour, making use of a number of other sciences such as anthropology, sociology, psychology, etc. (2) and (3) on the other hand display analytical-normative characteristics. They try to lay down what the contents of ethical behaviour should be. In the case of (2) the aim is to design a general and consistent system from which ethical action can be deduced (Kant is an outstanding example), while (3) is more concerned with applied ethics in trying to evolve a codex for moral behaviour in concrete situations.

As far as the positive sides of ethics and economics are concerned, no special problems arise, but certain complementary relations can be established. Since ethical norms can influence economic motives and behaviour, the economist will benefit from a knowledge of the contents and changes in ethical beliefs. Similarly, since changes in the economic environment leave their mark on ethical and moral views, the student of ethical dynamics can make use of the insights and prognoses of economic theorists. The problem of the ethical-economic connection (which will be the subject of subsequent chapters) has its roots in the normative aspects in both disciplines; this can make it more difficult to find a way to such peaceful coexistence.

To give an idea about the considerable range of normative ethics, it will be useful to start off with a number of groupings and distinctions which are common in the literature on moral philosophy. An important distinction which is closely connected with the historical trend from metaphysical to scientific world-views (Comte) is between absolute and non-absolute ethics. Absolute ethics postulate – as the adjective indicates – the existence of definite and permanent principles which are of universal validity and should be followed more or less unchanged at all times and in all places. Such principles might be advanced on 'rational' grounds, as exemplified in Kant's categorical imperative, or they may be based on transcendental, predominantly religious, thinking. Absolute ethics have the advantage of providing certainty with regard to the validity of norms, but occasionally they tend to suffer from a certain vagueness in content and from rigidity in a changing world.

Non-absolute ethics can be relative ethics on the one

hand and pluralistic ethics on the other, with possible overlaps between the two. Relative ethics are 'functional': their norms are derived from some targets lying beyond these norms, such as resting a justification for the norm of speaking the truth on the desire to have a reliable basis for social relations. When the final targets are changed, the ethical norms will also change. But since the targets behind the norms also contain value judgements which need justification, we are faced with an endless regress which must ultimately be terminated with an absolute rule. This will, however, often be facilitated by arriving at some principles which are generally accepted. Pluralistic approaches acknowledge the possibility of a variety of competing ethical systems stemming from different cultural environments. They can exist side-by-side without a possibility of dividing them into 'good' or 'bad', 'right' or 'wrong' systems. In non-absolute ethics the social consensus which is required for an effective ethical code can be obtained in a continuous process of finding a generally acceptable basis. This leads to the idea of a discoursive ethic (Habermas).

Relativism and pluralism are empirically important and have a greater capacity for adjustment and concrete relevance than absolute paradigms, but they contain seeds for ethical conflicts and can reduce the force of ethical norms. It should not be forgotten however that most ethical systems within a given cultural environment, be they absolute or relative, usually have quite a number of basic principles in common including altruism, rejection of brute force, distributive justice, etc. even though they may differ in less important matters. But usually there also exist some deviating ethical systems in outsider circles ('morals of thieves').

In addition to this basic distinction between absolute and non-absolute ethical systems, there exist other classifications which apply to both these systems. An important distinction is between an ethical belief based on conviction and a consequential ethic. With convictions as a base, one is looking for the 'good individual' who always follows the commands of his conscience however demanding they may be. A consequential ethic judges the goodness of an act by the effects it has. The difference between the two types can become quite considerable when one is faced with complex conditions and complicated cause-effect relationships. These problems have gained in importance in connection with ecological issues. The grave but distant effects which they involve have induced the philosopher H. Jonas to plead for an 'ethical principle of responsibility'.

The actions of the individual may be subjected to an act or to a rule system. In the first case an action is regarded as ethically right if the person in question has acted according to his ethical principles as they apply – in his view – to the concrete situation. Rule ethics on the other hand expect him or her to follow certain predetermined rules in certain situations. The agent's duty is only to determine which rule is applicable in a given situation. The advantages and disadvantages of the two systems, which may exist side-by-side, cannot be judged irrespective of the contents and quality of the personal norms and of the rules. In general it can be said that 'good' rules can have the advantage of taking into account wider consequences and of strengthening general behaviour but they run the danger of being too rigid in the face of new or unforeseen situations. This will lead to a breaking of rules or to an accumulation of exceptions. An individual act ethics is certainly more flexible, but it can suffer from too narrow a horizon, from errors and mistakes.

In concluding this by no means complete list of possible classifications of ethical theories, I want to mention the distinction between individual and social ethics which concerns the situations to be covered. While individual ethics deal with the ethical dimensions of individual actions, social ethics are concerned with the ethical qualities of the social framework, its institutions and its decisions.

This ends the overview of possible classifications of

systems of moral philosophy. There is no need to consider the special features of various systems. However there is one ethical philosophy which deserves a closer description before we say some words about critical-analytical approaches and about the notion of justice. The special philosophy I am thinking of is utilitarianism which can command particular attention because it had such a deep influence on the thinking of the classical economists and has remained an influence in later and modern developments.

Utilitarianism is a relatively wide and loosely-defined term which covers several aspects of philosophy. But it has a narrower and more clearly defined meaning when applied to ethical theory, which alone is of interest in our context. Though roots of utilitarianism can be traced back to early times, its main basis was laid in the 18th century, mainly by Jeremy Bentham who gave it a strong hedonistic bias. In the 19th century it was significantly extended and modified by John Stuart Mill. Since then it has remained a living element in ethical discussions and controversies.

Utilitarian ethics can adopt different forms, but a few basic ideas are common to all of them and can be summarized as follows. Utilitarian ethics – utilitarianism for short – is a rational, relative (functional) and consequential ethical system which can be applied to questions of individual and social ethics and can appear as act and/or rule utilitarianism. It is relative-functional because it does not refer back to an absolute idea of 'good' and 'bad' but judges the ethical quality of an action more or less exclusively by asking whether it serves (individually or as a rule) the aim of maximizing human happiness ('The greatest good of the greatest number'). It is consequential insofar as the moral quality of actions depends on the question as to what extent this aim has actually been achieved. This should be judged by an 'ethical calculus' which sets off pleasure against pain, 'happiness' against 'unhappiness', so as to arrive at a balance indicating whether human 'happiness' has increased or not. To increase or maximize the positive balance should be the essence of moral action. It can easily be seen that this maxim is equally applicable in individual and social ethics.

This rough sketch of the basic skeleton of utilitarian ethics throws up a host of complex questions which have provided continuous food for interpretations and developments in utilitarian discussions. Above all it is the vague idea of 'happiness' which gives rise to many differing interpretations. Is happiness a state of contentment or the result of current pleasurable and painful events? Is the aim pure hedonism, the satisfaction of every wish as it comes, or should preferences be weighted according to certain quality standards? How can the balance between pleasure and pain be calculated; how can it be compared between different persons? Should we welcome population growth because it will (so one hopes) increase the sum total of human happiness, or should we not rather aim at a maximum of per capita happiness? And what about the happiness of future generations?

As we see, many questions exist and many more could be added. If this were a book on ethics, all these questions would have to be discussed in detail. But for our purposes this is not necessary. The basic idea of utilitarianism in all its variations is relatively simple and plausible, and it is this basic idea which permeates economic thinking. Although economics is not directly concerned with happiness, pleasure and pain, etc., it does deal with needs, satisfaction and costs; the economic theorist's calculus of utility and costs reveals an obvious resemblance to the ethical calculus of the utilitarians. Added to this is the fact that utilitarianism more than many other ethical systems offers a guide to questions of social ethics. Questions of institutions, economic policy measures, etc. can be seen and judged on the basis of utilitarian principles.

Here we leave utilitarianism, whose influence on economics will come up in later chapters. But before we leave ethics altogether some observations of a 'positive' note should be added. So far we have dealt with the normative aspects of ethics and moral philosophy because these are the most relevant elements when it comes to a confrontation between ethics and valuations in economics. But philosophical studies also have their positive-critical branches which try to analyse the specifics of ethical statements and to point out in what respect they differ from other statements (including 'scientific' ones). These semantic studies, which have proliferated in the past 50 to 60 years (though their roots go back to Max Weber), have a certain relevance as a background to our subject. A short summary of these ideas therefore seems justified.

The point of departure is a distinction between three kinds of statements: statements about reality, desires and valuations. Statements about reality (e.g. 'it rains') rest on observations, induction or deduction and can be judged as true or false. This applies also to a statement like 'I believe that it rains' where the term 'believe' only serves to express uncertainty with regard to the truth of the statement. There may be divergences and conflicts with regard to such statements, but a 'rational' discourse and a convergence of views on the basis of objective facts is always possible, at least in principle. Statements of desires ('Open the window') are simply communications to other persons which cannot be subjected to a 'true/false' criterion. Finally we have value statements ('She is a good woman') which tell us something about the opinions and emotions of the speaker. These opinions and emotions are facts which can be explained (correctly or incorrectly). This is a task for the (positive) science *about* ethical beliefs. But the statement itself expresses merely a subjective view which cannot be described as true or false on any objective grounds. It is obvious that this supports the notion or the possibility of a pluralistic system of ethics.

Of course not every expression of an opinion has ethical characteristics. Ethical valuations are statements expressing opinions which touch 'important' questions of human relations.[4] What concerns us here is the distinction between factual, cognitive statements concerning objective realities ('is'-statements) and evaluative, emotive statements ('ought'-statements), with ethical statements falling into the second category. Only the cognitive statements can lead to true/false decisions. This 'rational' approach to ethics is not shared by transcendental philosophies which regard ethical values as fundamental objective truths which can be discovered in the same way as objective realities by a method of introspection and 'Verstehen' (understanding). This view cannot be accepted by rational analysis though it is of course recognized that *existing* ethical beliefs and norms are an objective reality whose influence and effects can be analysed scientifically, with significant insights for the social sciences (including economics).

While is seems easy enough to distinguish between cognitive and emotive statements as different specimens in principle, it is rather difficult to draw a sharp line when it comes to actual discourse. This is not only true for everyday language but applies also to scientific discussions. Cognitive and emotive elements, insights, desires and values are not easily separated in our thinking, and the problem is intensified through the fuzziness and the emotional associations of our language. Words like 'courageous', 'loyal', 'equilibrium', 'aggressive' etc. are a mixture of descriptive and evaluating content whose meaning and character cannot always be ascertained or kept in the 'proper' category. This is a problem which besets all social sciences.

In conclusion a word should be said about a special ethical category which will occupy us later on when we deal with problems of income distribution: the question of justice. Rights and justice are certainly to a large extent ethical phenomena, but ethical considerations do not necessarily include observations on justice. Thus utilitarianism has no special view on justice: human happiness is to be maximized but there is no rule about a 'just' distribution of happiness. Against this we find ethical philosophies which give highest priority to questions of justice. They try to develop norms (rights and duties) which will provide a secure basis for a 'just' order in the relations of a society ('distributive ethics' in the terms of Aristoteles). The idea of justice may be derived from some transcendental or religious principle (e.g. equality of all men and women) or it may be developed from 'rational' considerations. In the latter case a classical approach was (and is) the attempt to find norms on which a 'rational' population could agree unanimously in a pre-societal state of nature. Since assumptions about the conditions in such a pre-historic state and about human nature can vary considerably, it is not surprising that a wide variety of such societal agreements and 'just orders' has been created which already in the classical period ranged from the absolute monarchy of Hobbes to the universal democracy of Rousseau. In Chapter 9 we shall have occasion to return to this question.

Notes

1. D. L. Sills ed. (1968), *International Encyclopedia of the Social Sciences*, New York: Macmillan & Free Press, Vol. 5, p. 160.
2. In Chapter 4 we shall deal with the difference between ethical norms and other conventions.
3. The close relationship of the two terms is shown by the fact that ethics is the subject of moral philosophy.
4. In this respect we can distinguish ethical opinions from mere conventions like table manners etc. On this point see also Chapter 4.

2. Ethics and Economic Research

There are three different levels where ethics and economics can touch each other. As far as economic research as a whole is concerned – both theoretical and empirical – certain ethical rules concerning scientific research in general are relevant. They are widely accepted in the scientific community and will be treated immediately. At a second level we meet interrelationships between ethical theories and viewpoints on the one hand and the contents of 'positive' economic theories on the other. The explicit or implicit ethical elements of economic theories, as well as economic implications of ethical postulates, give rise to a number of questions and problems. These questions form the main content of this book. Finally there is a third level where applied ethics are confronted with different aspects of economic behaviour and institutions with the aim to develop realistic norms for ethical action. Typical for this field is the quickly spreading literature on business ethics and business culture which deals with the relations of business *vis-à-vis* customers and employees; but other branches also exist as for instance consumer ethics which deal with the responsibility of consumers in relation to ecological and social challenges. These diverse and specific applied ethics, with their various moral prescriptions (which – as business schools remind their students – may turn out to be quite profitable), will not be treated in this book.

As just mentioned, we first want to say some words on the ethics of scientific research in general because this also concerns economic research. The ethics of research consist of a set of more or less widely accepted rules of 'good' behaviour which apply particularly to scientific activities.

Deviations from these rules can be sanctioned by loss of prestige in the scientific community and beyond, and in serious cases can even lead to a loss of opportunities for further scientific work. These ethical standards of scientific research are not a clearly defined catalogue of norms, but consist of a number of guiding principles which are meant to foster the 'ethical' target of science, namely to achieve a continuous expansion of our knowledge of the world, a gradual approximation to 'truth' (however defined).

The 'fundamental rules' which a research ethics demand are fairly obvious and do not need any great elaboration. That all utterances should be 'true' and without any conscious falsification goes without saying. But it should also be the 'full truth'; that is one should publish all (relevant) results and not only those which support a preferred hypothesis. All collaborators and sources should always be named. As far as private information is used, the trust of the confiding person should not be abused. Published papers should not be published elsewhere without informing the reader about the previous publication.

In addition to these rather obvious basic norms, there exist several other less obvious questions which also involve ethical dilemmas. A very important and delicate problem concerns the question to what extent a researcher is (or should be) responsible for the possible effects of his research results. This problem came up with full force when the physicists who had developed the atom bomb were confronted with the disastrous results of the bombing of Hiroshima and Nagasaki. Like Oppenheimer, they had to ask themselves whether they could justify to themselves and others further research in this field even in a 'purely scientific' manner. Analogous problems can also arise in the social sciences, though the effects are normally not so dramatic or catastrophic. Thus a study of the effects of work organization and work control on the intensity of workers' efforts can be a 'purely objective' analysis. But its utilization may lead to greater stress and less work satisfaction for the work force than the researcher and others may regard as desirable. Such consequences should at least be considered by the scientist.

A famous concrete example illustrating this problem and concerning social sciences was a research project – the so-called CAMELOT Project – sponsored by the US army in 1964 programmed to find out what instruments could be used to forecast, to influence and to control social changes in Latin America. The ultimate aim was to make this research available to the CIA for its work in those countries. In the end the project had to be given up because the Norwegian sociologist Jan Galtung revealed the (secret) purpose of the programme and thus managed to kill it.

Another problem of responsibility arises in connection with the relations existing between the scientist and the persons or groups with whom he is involved in his research. This is particularly relevant in the social sciences where data and facts are required and obtained which may touch important interests and feelings of certain persons. Insofar as persons are questioned in the course of a research programme or included in experimental arrangements, they should not be misled about their role. A significant case in this respect was the famous Milgram experiment. This was an experimental study which tried to find out how far authority and obedience can modify individual responsibility and behaviour. Students were told to take part in an experiment to test how strong certain shocks must be to induce persons to give answers which they want to withhold. The experimental design was that the person to be tested sat in a glass cell and was asked questions. If the answer was not forthcoming, the student was told by the 'authority' (the experimenter) to press a lever which would transmit electric shocks of increasing intensity to the test person. The alleged purpose was to see at what point the resistance of the test person could be broken. In fact, however (but unknown to the students), there was no electricity involved at all. The persons in the cell simulated through increasing cries, wriggling, twisting, etc. a growing degree of suffering whenever the lever was moved. The true aim of the experiment was to see how far students would follow the commands of the expert even though their own feelings would revolt against inflicting pain on another human being. It is not important to report the results of this experiment here (ethically they were anything but gratifying). It is only mentioned as an example of a questionable research strategy which deceived the students and lured them, in the manner of an *agent provocateur*, into actions of which they were ashamed later on.

Some questions of an ethical nature are thrown up through the relations of scientific research with other spheres of life. In these days when research sponsored and contracted from private sources is becoming increasingly important, we are faced with the question of whether there may not arise a bias in the choice of research themes and in the perspective under which they are investigated. As a consequence other themes which from a societal point of view might be more relevant may be neglected. Questions of publication and free access to new knowledge have also to be considered when 'private' research is undertaken. The mere wish to keep open opportunities for further financial support can lead to a moral dilemma in deciding these questions.

While sponsoring carries a danger of suboptimal or biased publication (withholding some of the results), the opposite danger of an exaggerated interpretation of results – springing from prestige and the career interests of the scientists – has also to be considered. The desire to underline the importance and emphasize the positive elements of one's own research can come into conflict with the moral duty to present as full and as 'true' an account as possible both to one's colleagues and to the general public. Some reports of medical research results display the difficulties which researchers can experience in this respect.

The considerations in the preceding paragraphs should

suffice to indicate the contents and the range of questions regarding the ethics of research in general. We can now turn to our main subject, the relations between ethics and economic theory. The first question is of course whether such relations can be established. Or was the famous Austrian satirist Karl Kraus right when he wrote: 'You want to study business ethics? Then you must decide to do the one or the other.'

As far as the history of economic thought is concerned, Kraus was certainly wrong. Ethics and economics have a long common past. The philosophers and the early classicists who considered economic questions from antiquity till deep into the 19th century were almost always travelling on two roads. They approached their questions and problems from two angles: an ethical and a 'technical' one. The ethical element was based on the consideration of human needs and studied their regulation through political and economic institutions whose forms and consequences were subjected to ethical valuations. The 'technical' or 'engineering' element aimed at providing the state with necessary insights regarding the logistics of economic processes. It was efficiency-oriented without much regard for the ultimate aims to be achieved. This mixture of ethics and economic efficiency was already visible in Aristoteles's Trias (Politics – Economics – Ethics) and found its continuation in the scholastic philosophy of the Middle Ages. But also with Adam Smith, who in the 18th century presented the first major work (if not the beginning) of a comprehensive economic theory, ethics and economics are closely interlocked. This is not so surprising when we remember that Adam Smith was not only Professor of Economics but also – and not incidentally – Professor of Moral Philosophy. Even before he wrote his path-breaking *The Wealth of Nations* he had written a *Theory of Moral Sentiments*, and many ideas of this earlier work were mirrored in his magnum opus.

The parting of ways came only in the course of the

19th century under the influence of enlightenment and the enormous advances achieved in the natural sciences whose dynamics became the driving force of industrial capitalism. The success of the natural sciences in general and of physics in particular, together with the new problems thrown up by the complexities of a highly differentiated market economy, induced a strong trend in the direction of 'scientifying' the social sciences, of formalizing their 'technical' aspects; in short of turning them into pure 'positive' theories. For the French sociologist Comte this was a decisive new stage in the development of social science.

This 'scientification' of economics, which had already become visible in Ricardo and which (in the 19th century) reached a climax in the general equilibrium theory of Walras, has led to a separation of economics from its ethical roots. The 'mainstream economics' of the 20th century fully accepts this separation. Economic theory is seen as a positive science which has to analyse and to explain the mechanisms of economic processes. It has to restrict itself to cognitive statements. Important as ethical valuations ('ought'-statements) may be, they should not form part of the economist's research programme.

This postulate of 'Wertfreiheit' (freedom from value statements),[1] with its implication of a sharp division between 'purely' economic statements on the one hand and ethical statements on the other, will be treated in some detail in the following chapter. But quite apart from the view one takes with regard to this postulate, one is faced with the fact that – explicitly or implicitly, consciously or unintended – evaluating sentences appear again and again in the theoretical writings of economists. This explains why there has always been room for ideological analyses of economic theories; Myrdal's classical study of 1932 on the political element in the development of economic theory presents an outstanding example.[2] The 'intrusion' of ethical elements into various segments of economic theory will be the subject of subsequent chapters. At this stage we restrict ourselves to two further general remarks.

The first is a reminder that there are some economists who do not share the general view regarding the predominantly positive character of economic theory. For them the problems discussed in this book – the dilemmas and contradictions arising from a postulate of Wertfreiheit confronted with ethical interjections in practice – are not relevant. They oppose the dominant view not only because a separation of factual and ethical elements may be difficult; they regard it as misdirected in principle because they feel that economic and ethical elements are so closely interconnected that a separation of the two should be avoided.[3] For theories of this sort a dissection of hidden ethical notions does not make sense. On methodological grounds they have to be judged as wholesale alternatives to mainstream economics.

The second remark refers to an increasing interest in problems of economic-ethical interfaces in recent times. Several factors have contributed to a greater readiness for interdisciplinary contacts. The ecological problem has sharpened sensibilities to questions of social responsibility which cannot be sufficiently covered by a purely economic analysis, and similar questions are raised by the conflicts between technical and human aspects in a world of accelerating technological change. Problems of institutional change and adjustments in the economic framework seem to demand a wider perspective. At the same time ethics can obviously profit by learning from the economist's decision theory. Deciding between 'good' and 'bad' occupies a central place in ethics and this area can benefit from the high formal qualities which economic theories of rational choice have achieved. Conversely, economists concerned with the concrete substance of economic motives and preferences can benefit from paying attention to contents, forms and effects of ethical factors which lie behind those preferences.

An article by Melvin Reder[4] may be used as a simple

example of a formal attempt to combine moral and economic elements in a theory of production. Reder wants to show that widely accepted ethical norms can present a factor of productive efficiency and should be treated as such. As an example he chooses a specific moral norm M containing the rule 'Keep your word' (or 'Meet your obligations without cheating'). Such a norm is of relevance in economic life because a large part of economic transactions does not consist of direct exchange but covers future obligations (credit, labour contracts, delayed deliveries, etc.) whose fulfilment is uncertain. This can lead to costs and losses which can be reduced through moral behaviour.

As a concrete example let us take the case of credit. The debtor has a financial interest not to repay the credited sum as long as his gain from default is not wiped out by costs of litigation, loss of good will in future transactions, etc. Yet adherence to the moral norm M (defined above) can prevent him from defaulting even when it is profitable. In terms of utility analysis we can use a function $U = U(W, X_1, X_2 \ldots)$ where U stands for utility, W for wealth (including discounted future income), and $X_1, X_2 \ldots$ for other relevant factors including moral norms like M. Adherence to M will be a source of satisfaction (good conscience, good reputation, etc.). But a trade-off between M and W creates a decision problem. Ethical behaviour has its costs and this means that one has to decide how high a moral stance one wants to afford.

Reder now suggests that we define with M the *intensity* (and/or frequency) with which the moral norm is used and that this intensity of moral effort can be expressed as a function of W, the wealth of a person, and a sum S, which is the maximum amount she or he is prepared to forego in order to fulfil a given contract. This yields the function $M = M(W, S)$ with $M_W < 0$ and $M_S > 0$.[5] This means that a greater moral strength is indicated, the greater the (financial) sacrifice one is prepared to accept, but that a given sacrifice weighs less the greater the wealth one possesses. The simplest form such an index of moral strength could take would be $M = \frac{S}{W}$.

The stronger the *M*s in different persons and the greater the number of persons covered, the greater will be the confidence in a given economic community that contracts will be honoured and credits repaid. Opportunities for future-oriented contracts are increased; fewer resources have to be used for information, controls, litigation, etc., and risks are reduced all round. Thus ethical behaviour can become an (economic) factor of production which increases the efficiency of economic processes or even becomes a precondition for some transactions. Yet a difficulty remains. Like in many other macroeconomic-ethical relations, we have here a case of 'prisoners' dilemma' as we know it from game theory. While it is in the interest of everybody and of society as a whole that all citizens should adhere to the moral norm, it 'pays' the individual to break the norm at least from time to time. Thus if individual financial interests prevail, the effective moral environment cannot materialize. Common action may be required to establish it through education, socialization, public opinion, etc. Such measures of ethical improvement can then be seen – from an economic point of view – as efficiency-improving investments.

Notes

1. 'Wertfreiheit' which stands for 'Werturteilsfreiheit' is a term which played an eminent role in methodological discussions in Germany and Austria at the turn of the last century (see Chapter 3). There seems to be no short English term to take its place.
2. The original work appeared in German (*Das politische Element in der nationalökonomischen Doktrinbildung*). English translation: *The Political Element in the Development of Economic Theory*, London: Routledge (1953).
3. A recent attempt to design such a closely integrated economic-

ethical framework is contained in P. Koslowski (1988), *Prinzipien der Ethischen Ökonomie*, Tübingen: J.C.B. Mohr.

4. M. Reder (1979), 'The Place of Ethics in the Theory of Production' in M. J. Boskin (ed.), *Economics and Human Welfare. Essays in Honour of Tibor Scitovsky*, New York: Academic Press.
5. M_W is the partial derivative of the function $M(.)$ in relation to W: $\frac{\delta M}{\delta W}$. Similarly for M_S.

3. The 'Wertfreiheits' Problem

In this chapter we want to take a closer look at the postulate of 'Wertfreiheit' that was mentioned above. As we have seen it demands the complete banishment of valuating statements in scientific analyses. This view, which has a strong hold on the social science community, has a long history and was the subject of hot discussions particularly among German-speaking economists at the end of the 19th and the beginning of the 20th century. On the one side were the analytical-theoretical economists who shaped their old Ricardian and their new marginal theories in the image of the natural sciences, with observation, analysis, experiment and test as desired instruments; on the other side those social scientists gathered who had a more philosophical and historical background and who tended to the opinion that the human sciences were a completely different category demanding a special methodology. Instead of trying to obtain empirical regularities and general theoretical 'laws' like the natural sciences, the human sciences (including economics) – so it was argued – should try to discover the 'essence' of society and of the economy by description, introspection and 'understanding'. 'Understanding' would give access to insights about the quality of developments, whether they are 'good' (conforming to the 'essence' of the economy) or 'undesirable' (not conforming). Valuations in this view are part and parcel of an 'objective' study of the economy and its 'essence'.

This methodological dispute, which is indicated here only in rough outline leaving out all its ramifications, touched the research strategy of all social sciences. In economics this dispute reached a climax in a famous methodological confrontation in the late 19th century between the leading German economic historian Gustav Schmoller and Carl Menger, the Austrian co-founder of the marginalist school. Though the 'Wertfreiheit'-question was not explicitly mentioned in this dispute, it was implicitly present in the juxtaposition of Menger's strictly empirical-analytical-deductive position[1] and Schmoller's defence of an historical-understanding-valuating perspective. This dispute triggered off a serious division in the leading German-speaking economic society (the *Verein für Socialpolitik*) in which the Wertfreiheit-question became a central subject. These discussions were decisively influenced by Max Weber's strong advocacy in favour of adopting the Wertfreiheit-postulate. On this question he has remained an important influence to this day. In the hands of his followers, however, his differentiated analysis (which fully recognizes various difficulties of the principle) has often been simplified to an absolute dogma of Wertfreiheit.

What quality should be accorded to this Wertfreiheit-principle? What are the arguments in its favour and what problems are connected with it? As we have seen in its simplest form it demands a strict separation of empirical-logical, cognitive statements from all 'non-scientific' subjective value elements. This does of course not mean that the scientist should not be allowed to express personal opinions. The rule only applies to statements made in his role as a scientist, i.e. in his scientific work.

Simple as this principle may appear, it contains quite a number of complications and difficulties. To begin with we should be quite clear that the Wertfreiheit-postulate, the demand to abstain from value judgements, is itself a value judgement with regard to 'desirable' qualities in scientific methodology.[2] Later I shall argue why I favour a (modified) acceptance of the principle (a subjective opinion!) for various reasons. But it cannot be derived from any *essential* aspects of scientific research. One can of course *define* science in such a way that valuations are excluded, but there exists no 'essence' of science which would forbid the use of other definitions.

But even when one is prepared to accept the postulate, a number of difficulties arise. First of all some degree of valuation enters quite unavoidably at the start of every research project even though the scientist may not be aware of it. The choice of one's field of study itself involves general ideas about the purpose of these activities (such as the discovery of truth, career, social relevance) and some of these motivations will have ethical connotations. Similar questions arise when concrete themes are chosen, as well as the perspective under which they are to be considered. Why was a certain theme chosen and not another one? Why was a certain aspect regarded as a problem worth studying? Even in the choice of methods, certain valuations may play a role. When for instance in an empirical study about income structures a choice has to be made between using either absolute or relative income differentials, this choice may well be influenced by some subjective 'feeling' about the importance of absolute or relative positions for individuals and social groups. And in addition to all this, the ethical principles regarding research in general which we considered earlier are also relevant.

The ethical aspects which have just been enumerated will affect the work of the scientist quite irrespective of whether or not he accepts the Wertfreiheit-principle. This is unavoidable. But in addition there may also be good reasons to go beyond these 'endogenous' value elements and to include some ethical valuations quite deliberately. One good reason which is rather unproblematic is the 'objective' presentation of ethical values which are related to the economic processes and theoretical results and which could influence their interpretation and utilization. If this is done in a fair manner, presenting the various possible alternatives, such an extension of a 'purely' economic perspective can yield additional insights and aid the decision-maker without getting research itself implicated in recommending specific actions. This does not cause any particular problems.

Such problems turn up, however, when the research displays a certain endogenous value bias. This will show up in an uneven or consciously incomplete enumeration of potential alternatives, in bringing some of them into closer contact with the analysis and in implicit or explicit tendencies to apply valuative-emotional adjectives like 'good', 'bad', 'desirable' or 'optimal' to certain constellations and results. This is the central and relevant aspect of the Wertfreiheit-problem; it is also the one aspect which Max Weber had mainly in mind. His admonitions were above all directed against misuses which can arise when social scientists – and particularly university teachers and other pedagogues – get their ethical and political opinions mixed up with their expert knowledge. Their personal opinions should not be allowed to gain special weight by receiving the imprint of expert prestige. This danger could be excluded if the scientist *qua* scientist restricted himself to factual statements and 'value-free' theories.

Though such a demand for Wertfreiheit is easily understandable, it turns out to be rather difficult to adhere to it in practice. Scientists are after all also (!) human beings whose thinking and whose language are influenced by cognitive *and* emotional elements which are not easily separable. Moreover, they may be driven to devote special attention to certain questions in consequence of ethical beliefs which may be regarded as highly laudable. Under such circumstances it is perhaps too much to expect scientists always to be able to distinguish quite clearly between 'is' and 'ought' or to strictly exclude all normative nuances in their studies. In view of these difficulties, to which have to be added the previously mentioned unavoidable valuative elements, a number of economists and other social scientists (among them above all Gunnar Myrdal and Paul Streeten) have advocated a modified approach to the problem. Since absolute Wertfreiheit is impossible it might be better to admit – and in many cases even welcome – that ethical-emotional elements do enter the analytical work, but to make it at the same time a 'duty' for scientists to declare openly and explicitly what the value premises are which have influenced them in the choice of their themes and perspectives and which underlie the normative elements which have (with or without intention) crept into their theories. Under no circumstances should such normative, emotive statements be presented in a pseudo-scientific wrapping.

A further ethical aspect of Wertfreiheit which concerns the economist more than his theoretical work presents itself when the economist acts as expert or adviser to public bodies. Should he regard himself as a 'value-free' expert ('social engineer') who gives the ruling governments (of whatever colour) 'best technical' advice on how to achieve the various targets they have set themselves? Or should he try – when asked for advice – to combine his technical knowledge with such norms as he regards as ethically binding? Perhaps he should serve only those governments whose normative values he shares. Or perhaps he should refrain altogether from advising governments and see his duty in making his expert knowledge available to the public instead, thus contributing through a presentation of various potential alternatives and their economic and ethical implications to a better foundation for critical democratic decisions. Several paths can thus be taken and it will depend on individual ethical positions which one will be chosen. But whichever path it is, the Wertfreiheit-principle – be it of the Weber-type or the Myrdal-type – requires that evaluative, personal elements should not be clothed as 'scientific' or theoretical expert knowledge.

What are the conclusions to which these considerations lead, or – better phrased – what are the consequences I personally would recommend? Quite generally I think that Weber's postulate that scientific theorizing should aim at a value-free presentation is a useful principle. It helps to keep scientific debates relatively free from emotions; it offers opportunities for interpersonal comparisons of results, and it shuts out fruitless conflicts about 'oughts'. But the principle must not be interpreted too strictly because value elements cannot be banished altogether. This leads to the additional demand that value preferences and value elements should be laid open. If this is done the 'scientific nature' of any analysis is not threatened even if value judgements turn up now and then. In addition to these ideas which refer to the ethics of research, one can also demand or expect from scientists (as from other persons) a generally high ethical standard which should also be reflected in the subjects of his research and in his private recommendations of certain actions based on research results. This can lead to an ethical conflict for the scientist. In his role as a 'scientist' he should feel obliged to give as full and as true an account of all his research results as possible; on the other hand, a less complete or even somewhat biased presentation might be able to encourage actions and situations which his 'private ethics' regard as good and desirable. This is a genuine ethical dilemma. But conflicts between ethical norms are not exceptional; they constitute an essential aspect of ethical decision problems.[3]

Notes

1. His views were presented in his book *Untersuchungen über die Methode der Socialwissenschaften und der politischen Ökonomie insbesondere* (1883). English translation: *Problems of Economics and Sociology*, Urbana: University of Illinois Press (1963).
2. This fact seems to land us in a paradox. 'Science should be wertfrei' is itself a Werturteil. If the scientist declares that he accepts this principle he does in fact introduce a Werturteil and therefore acts unscientifically. If, on the other hand, he refrains from explicitly accepting the principle then he could also accept it as a scientist (because then value judgements are permitted). The seeming paradox vanishes when we note that the Werturteil-postulate belongs to a different level (a meta-level) separated from the science sphere. It is a (value-)statement *about* scientific statements but not itself a part of them.

3. In lectures on moral philosophy which I attended as a student our Professor wanted to explain to us the nature of a moral problem. 'If you take out your wife on a boating excursion', he said, 'and she falls into the water you will jump into the water and save her. This is not a moral problem. But when you undertake the excursion with your wife and your mother-in-law and both of them fall into the water, then you are faced with a moral problem.'

4. Homo Oeconomicus – Homo Sociologicus

Ethically relevant questions and misunderstandings arise in connection with some basic economic notions and assumptions even before questions of theories and their interpretations come into play. Two questions are particularly prominent in this context: the specific conception of the individual as an economic agent and the role of the market as a central institution in the economic process. Both these elements play an important role in the basic framework of 'mainstream economics'. In this chapter we deal with the role of the individual. Some remarks on the ethical aspects of the market follow in the next chapter.

One of the most decisive creations of microeconomic theory is the model of the 'rational individual', the homo oeconomicus. It provides a rich soil for theoretical analyses and for the interpretation of individual economic decisions and actions. Under the obvious influence of utilitarian ideas, the homo oeconomicus is 'constructed' as a person whose (sole) endeavour is to satisfy his subjective preferences (which are assumed to be given) in such a way that – given the constraints of time and budget limitations – a maximum of utility is obtained. With the additional assumption of a high level of information about external conditions, one obtains an individual who will be able – depending on his wealth and the prices in the market – to calculate 'rationally' what economic decisions (purchase of goods, labour supply, etc.) will yield an optimal result. When this model of man is combined with a few further assumptions (in particular the 'psychological law' of declining marginal utility), one obtains an extremely pliable instrument for dealing theoretically with individual actions and reactions in a changing market environment.

From time to time one meets ethical objections to the homo oeconomicus; these we can dismiss quite easily because they rest on a misunderstanding. In non-economic circles, but occasionally also among economists themselves, it is sometimes argued that the 'type' of the homo oeconomicus must be rejected because it is a distortion of the image of man. The homo oeconomicus who is bent on nothing but maximizing satisfactions should be rejected both on factual and ethical grounds: the model idealizes and generalizes, so it is said, the absolute egotist and does not consider the 'good' characteristics of man, his or her capacity for altruistic feelings, for sympathy and empathy.

Such moral objections against the homo oeconomicus rest on two misunderstandings. The first concerns the formal character of the underlying hypothesis of satisfaction maximization. This hypothesis does not imply egotistic or hedonistic behaviour. All it means is the assumption that people will try to satisfy their preferences (optimally) without asserting anything about the contents of those preferences.[1] They may be of an egotistic nature but they can just as well be directed towards altruistic aims. Maximization of satisfaction will then lead to altruistic behaviour.

The second misunderstanding has to do with actual decision-making. The homo oeconomicus is rejected by some because it is seen to present a wrong and misleading presentation of the ways people arrive at their decisions in real life. The misunderstanding here is the assumption that the homo oeconomicus is meant to present a 'true' image of real persons. This is not the case. The model of the homo oeconomicus is a theoretical construction, an abstraction and accentuation of certain aspects of human motivation and decision-making which are regarded as particularly relevant in the realm of economic transactions. This excuses the neglect of other modes of behaviour which in the marketplace are less important. The justification of the homo oeconomicus assumption does not therefore rest on its realism with regard to human nature, but on the question of whether it provides a satisfactory instrument for dealing with decisions in the economic sphere. Even if one believes that human motivations and human actions need a far wider and more sophisticated explanatory basis than that presented by the 'rational maximization algorithm' of the homo oeconomicus, one should admit that this 'reduced' hypothesis shows sufficient parallels to market behaviour and economic decision-making to be serviceable as an instrument in economic analysis.[2]

Moral objections to the homo oeconomicus are thus not justified. But other problems remain. The argument that the homo oeconomicus does not mirror the totality of real persons has been admitted but shown to be irrelevant. But the question remains whether the model is *factually* sufficient even when we restrict ourselves to the economic sphere. After all economic actions are part of our general life even though they display certain special characteristics. The people who act in the economic sphere are the same people who are engaged in all sorts of non-economic dealings, and it seems unlikely that their motives and decision processes will always completely change when they move from one sphere to the other. Just as the 'rational' calculations of the homo oeconomicus may be relevant in non-economic situations of conflicting preferences (when for instance I have to decide whether to go out with my friend *A* or my friend *B*), other forms of decision-making which are typical in non-economic spheres may play a role in economic circumstances.

A significant model competing with that of homo oeconomicus is the homo sociologicus, the abstraction favoured by sociologists. In contrast to the economic method which centres on the isolated individual and his/her choices, the sociological perspective looks at the individual as part of society, at his 'embeddedness' in the social environment and its challenges. In this environment, persons take on certain 'roles' and try to conform to socially determined and sanctioned norms which as a rule they accept and make guide-posts for their actions. While the actions of the homo oeconomicus are purposeful and future-oriented ('If you want *Y* do *X*'), the norms of the homo sociologicus are not directed towards results but – dependent on the situation – are prescriptions for 'proper' action ('Do *X*' or 'Don't do *X*' or 'If you do *Y* then also do *X*').

Norm-oriented behaviour also appears in economic relations and is of relevance to our discussion because many – though certainly not all – norms contain moral and ethical elements. As far as norm-oriented behaviour affects economic actions, the assumption of the homo oeconomicus leads to a neglect or false interpretation of some behaviour patterns and their consequences.[3] Examples of such alternative patterns are for instance considerations of 'fairness' in economic decisions,[4] replacing purely individual maximization, ethical arguments and concessions in wage negotiations. The fact that norms containing ethical elements can play a role in economic processes but are usually neglected in economic theory justifies a short consideration of norms and some of their aspects.

Norm-oriented behaviour differs from the target-oriented behaviour of the homo oeconomicus in following certain rules rather than looking for the 'best' strategy to arrive at a certain goal. Various motives are at work which secure the application of such rules even if they are not (legally or otherwise) binding, and could include satisfaction, fear, shame, etc. But not every rule-dominated action is a norm and not every norm has ethical characteristics. A few distinctions are in order.

Rule-dominated repetitive behaviour in the face of a changing environment can be involuntary: it can be due to illness (compulsion neurosis) or to strictly enforced laws. These cases are hardly of interest as far as decision theory is concerned. Another important case of repetitive action is habitual behaviour. This is obviously quite widespread in economic life. Not every change and least of all small changes in the economic environment induce persons to rearrange the pattern of their 'normal' behaviour (such as expenditure patterns). One can perhaps accuse economic theory of paying too little attention to the importance of habitual rigidity. But the phenomenon as such can easily be fitted into the framework of the homo oeconomicus model if we regard adjustments – however small – as 'costs' (time, money, nuisance, etc.). Habitual behaviour can then be seen as an efficient utility-maximizing strategy where the 'costs' of adjustment are set against the advantages one could derive from continuous adaptation to circumstances.

Norms, however, do not derive their validity and durability from such an individual and flexible utility calculation. They are socially accepted constants to which one tries to adhere even in the face of strong inducements to act differently. These norms can be further divided into conventions and norms in a narrower sense.

Conventions are rules of social behaviour which are not prescribed by law but are practised because they prove to be useful. Walking on the left side (or right side, as the case may be) of crowded streets or staircases is an example. Though there are no laws demanding such action and though it might sometimes be more convenient or quicker to use the other side, most people will stick to the convention. And this is 'rational' because the *general acceptance* of this principle will normally be efficient; the single individual is capable of acknowledging the usefulness of such collective behaviour. The widespread acceptance of conventions provides a solution to the 'prisoners' dilemma' that would exist in the absence of such a convention. Then it might be *individually* rational to walk against the stream or to follow no definite rule. But this would result in 'chaotic' conditions under which all would suffer. Yet this could not be repaired by a *single* individual adopting the rule of walking on one side only; a general convention is needed. Conventions can be the result of explicit declarations or of an evolutionary process. Once a potentially useful collective practice has got hold of a number of persons for some reason or another, a process of diffusion and intensification can set in which ultimately results in a widely accepted convention.[5]

Conventions ultimately derive their validity only from their original usefulness (which may get lost in the course of time). Norms in the narrower sense of the word (simply 'norms' in what follows), on the other hand, are not or at least not exclusively based on considerations of usefulness. They are followed because normative behaviour as such is regarded as binding. To obey the norm or to break it produces such emotions as joy, anguish or shame in the norm-oriented person which cannot be reduced to a purely 'rational' calculus of gains and losses. Such norms cover a wide field. They reach from 'good manners' which may signal attachment to a certain social group to fundamental ethical commandments. These latter types, the ethical norms, are linked to our subject of ethics and economic theory. While it cannot be the task of economic theory to investigate the origins, contents and diffusion of ethical norms, there are good reasons for giving greater consideration to their role and influence than has been usual so far. Such consideration could modify and enrich the one-sided decision model of economic theory. The following diagram, taken from a paper by Jon Elster,[6] is a rough indication of the structure which such an extended decision model could take.

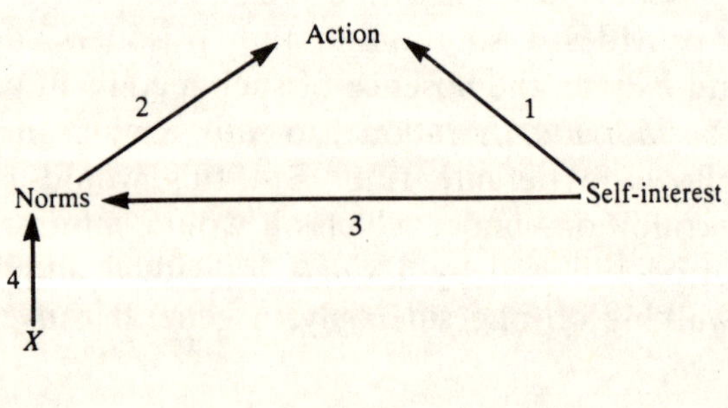

In this diagram X stands for the original factors leading to the evolution and diffusion of ethical norms. Ethical theory is mainly concerned with branches (3) and (4), sociologists with (2) and economists mainly with (1).[7] A more comprehensive approach combining the different branches could prove fruitful. As an example of a rather preliminary attempt at establishing a *formal* link between the homo oeconomicus and the homo sociologicus, a paper by Lindenberg[8] can serve as an illustration.

Lindenberg's intention is to design a model for confronting the homo oeconomicus with the homo sociologicus, or in other words 'interests' which are target- and situation-oriented with 'morals' which fix duties in an absolute manner. Interests and morals can come into conflict and this should be mirrored in the decision process.

Lindenberg's model is designed for the analysis of decision patterns over longer periods when interests and morals can be effective in various proportions. For instance there can be many distributions of punctual and late arrivals at work within a year. The model should explain (in the tradition of the economist) the 'rational' choice of the individual as to how to distribute such conflicting motives over time. For this purpose Lindenberg uses a 'discrimination model'.

To indicate the nature of such a model we first look at a simple example. We assume the existence of two 'utility baskets', K_1 and K_2. The main basket K_1 corresponds to the normal utility calculus and shows the utilities of certain results (such as profits) which can be obtained in various alternative ways. The side basket K_2 contains utilities which I can derive from a *distribution* of alternatives in a given period. We shall use the term 'strategy' for the chosen pattern of alternative actions. A simple example can illustrate this approach. Let us assume there are two machines, A and B, which at the pressing of a lever deliver £100 with different probabilities. With A the probability of success is 0.7, with B only 0.4. Now take a person who is allowed to operate these machines for some time. We assume that his or her main interest lies in obtaining the highest possible sum of money. The utility of that sum is contained in basket K_1. But there may also be a 'taste' for variation; using the same machine all the time may become boring. Although machine *A* is more productive than *B* in producing money, some satisfaction may also be derived from using *B* at least from time to time. The utility obtained from this *variation* in behaviour is contained in basket K_2. Total utility is then the result of both effects: the final amount of money and the degree of variation.

Using this example we can lay down certain definitions:

- *Pure* strategies are those which are directed exclusively at the main target (K_1). In our example this would mean that only machine *A* is operated.
- *Mixed* strategies take account of the desire for variation: basket K_2 is also included. In our example this means that *B* is also occasionally used. The sum of money will be lower than in the case of a pure strategy but total utility can be higher.

In addition to this division one can also distinguish between discriminatory and non-discriminatory strategies (hence the term 'discrimination model'):

- *Non-discriminating* strategies are those where all alternatives have an equal chance of being used. In our example this means that both *A* and *B* have a chance of 0.5 to go into operation.
- *Discriminating* strategies are those in which some alternatives obtain a certain priority. A pure strategy (only *A*) is therefore a case of total discrimination.

Building on these elements we now construct within the traditional economic assumption of 'rational' maximization a 'moral-containing' discrimination model. As in the previous example we distinguish two alternatives: a 'main target' and a 'desire for variation'. A strategy S is characterized by the mixture in which the alternatives A_1 and A_2 are used, with A_1 denoting the alternative which gives better results for the main target. P_1 will be used to denote the relative frequency with which A_1 is used and $P_2 = 1 - P_1$ is the corresponding frequency for the 'variation activity' A_2. P_1 (and P_2) characterize the chosen strategy. Since we regard A_1 as serving the *main* target, we shall assume that $P_1 \geqslant P_2$. (In the case of $P_1 = P_2$ there is no discrimination.)

For every strategy, with P_1, P_2 (i.e. the degree of discrimination) given, we have

$$E(U_S) = E(U_D) - DU_D \qquad (4.1)$$

where E stands for expected utility, U_S for the utility of the chosen strategy S, U_D for the utility of the results obtained for the main target (with D for degree of discrimination), and DU_D for the loss in utility following from discrimination (reduction in variation). As D increases (with growing P_1) both the main results and U_D also increase, but so does the item DU_D which is subtracted.

Equation (4.1) can be further expanded. For $E(U_D)$ we can write

$$E(U_D) = ag_1P_1 + ag_2\,(1 - P_1) = a(g_1 - g_2)\,P_1 + ag_2 \qquad (4.2)$$

with a for the marginal utility of the main target (e.g. money), and g_1 and g_2 for the amounts of the main target which are delivered by alternatives A_1 or A_2 (with $g_1 > g_2$). For the loss of utility caused through discrimination (loss of variation), we introduce the following quadratic loss function.

$$DU_D = (P_1 - 0.5)^2,\ P_1 \geqslant P_2 \qquad (4.3)$$

Since non-discrimination is characterized by $P_1 = 0.5$, the formula indicates that loss of utility only begins when discrimination ('one-sidedness') sets in. It rises with rising discrimination.

Combining (4.1), (4.2) and (4.3) we obtain

$$E(U_S) = a(g_1 - g_2)\, P_1 + ag_2 - (P_1 - 0.5)^2 \quad (4.4)$$

Utility maximization demands a determination of the optimal degree of discrimination characterized by an optimal $P_1 = P_1^*$. Differentiating (4.4) with regard to P_1 and maximizing we obtain

$$\frac{dE(U_S)}{dP_1} = a(g_1 - g_2) - 2\,(P_1 - 0.5)^2 \underset{\text{max!}}{=} 0 \quad (4.5)$$

$$P_1^* = \frac{a}{2}\,(g_1 - g_2) + 0.5 \quad (4.6)$$

On the assumption that A_1 is more productive with regard to the main target than A_2 ($g_1 > g_2$), we obtain a discrimination in favour of A_1 ($P_1 > 0.5$) which is higher the greater the difference between the two 'productivities'. Where no such difference exists ($g_1 = g_2$), the strategy becomes non-discriminating ($P_1^* = 0.5$).

We now turn to an application of this discrimination model to the problem of interests versus morals. We introduce a moral rule *R* which prescribes certain actions in certain situations. 'Moral' persons feel a certain obligation to obey this rule. In the course of repetitive situations, the person has to decide in each individual instance whether to stick to the rule or to break it. Application of the rule (conformity) will add to utility; non-conformity will cause disutility. Moral behaviour is thus not an absolute behavioural constant but is submitted to the calculus of utility. If moral behaviour demands big sacrifices, one may be prepared to break the rule in spite of the disutility such 'sins' cause.

Let us now look at a 'moral' person to whom conformity to moral norms means a lot (homo sociologicus). We assume – in the framework of our model – that moral behaviour is his *main* target, while other aims (such as making money) are the 'side issue'. Moral conformity is therefore placed in basket K_1. In each situation the person is faced with the alternatives of either sticking to the rule or breaking it. To simplify matters one can assume that conformity to R brings an addition to utility of +1 while non-conformity leads to a corresponding loss (−1). These are the values corresponding to g_1 and g_2. Consequently we obtain from equation (4.6) the following 'optimal' strategy for repetitive actions:

$$P_1^* = \frac{a}{2}[1 - (-1)] + 0.5 = \mathrm{a} + 0.5. \qquad (4.7)$$

Here a represents the marginal utility of moral action. The higher this utility (the higher a), the higher the value of P_1^*; that is, the greater the discrimination in favour of moral conformity.

It may seem strange that in equation (4.7) no reference is made to basket K_2; there seems to be no consideration of the utilities of the 'side issue' (making money). But this information does not appear explicitly because we have chosen a very simplified structure of the model. In fact the utility of the alternative action is implicitly contained in the factor a. The marginal utility of moral conformity is not independent of the intensity of alternative needs or desires. If for instance the need for more money increases, the marginal utility of money will rise at the cost of the marginal utility of moral behaviour; a will decline and with it P_1^* so that deviations from moral behaviour (in favour of A_2) will become more frequent. If the pressure of the alternative aims becomes so strong that special (additional) morality can no longer be 'afforded', a will be reduced to zero, $P_1^* = 0.5$ and the strategy will become non-discriminating. Moral behaviour will have lost its priority. Finally the other aim (money) may become so important that it overshadows moral feelings ('immoral person'). Money now moves into basket K_1, morals into basket K_2, and actions are discriminated in favour of 'unscrupulous' money-making with occasional moral excursions in order to reduce the utility losses springing from a bad conscience.

It would be wrong to expect too much from such a simple model. It cannot by itself provide any deep new insights. But it does help to show that norm-oriented ethical behaviour can – if this is to be the intention – be integrated into the economist's utility maximization framework. However, additional considerations are required if justice is to be done to the special decisional conflicts that can arise. Even this simple model indicates why ethical norms are sometimes being followed in spite of changes in economic circumstances, while at the same time these same norms may not be consistently followed even when circumstances are fairly stable.

Notes

1. The deliberate abstinence from dealing with the contents and changes of preferences is certainly a weak spot in economic theories and reduces their analytical impact and their applicability. In this respect a wide field is open for interdisciplinary cooperation between economists, biologists, psychologists etc.
2. On the other hand it seems a doubtful method when economists and others practise 'economic imperialism' trying to sell their model of homo oeconomicus to other social sciences and spheres of life.
3. In a purely formal way this problem could be circumvented by making norm-obedience a personal preference. Normative behaviour would then coincide with maximizing preference satisfaction. But this would turn the rational maximization hypothesis into a mere tautology. Any action whatsoever could be interpreted as a contribution to optimal satisfaction. And sentences like 'I should

very much like to rob *X* of his computer, but this is not done' would not make much sense.

4. See Chapter 9.
5. The evolution of more formal institutions can often be explained in a similar manner; also institutions might evolve directly from conventions. Such processes are an important element in institutional and evolutionary economic theories.
6. J. Elster (1989), 'Social Norms and Economic Theory', *Journal of Economic Perspectives*, 3 (4), Fall.
7. A somewhat similar distinction is supplied by Sen who distinguishes between two motives for action: (1) 'agency' and (2) 'well-being'. Agency refers to goals and values outside oneself (altruism, groups, nation) while well-being is concentrated on one's own happiness and satisfaction. The two motives are interdependent. Agency acts can increase well-being, but they can also reduce well-being. Economic theory neglects agency or it considers it only as far as its effects increase well-being. The conflict aspect is neglected. See A. Sen (1987), *On Ethics and Economics*, Oxford: Blackwell, p. 41.
8. S. Lindenberg (1983), 'Utility and Morality', *Kyklos*, **36** (3), September.

5. Moral Aspects of the Market

Markets which are characterized, at least partly and with differing intensity, by free contracting, flexible prices and by competition perform a decisive instrumental function in a modern monetary economy. They prove to be essential for the coordination of the millions of decisions required in production and consumption, for the allocation of capital, labour and raw materials in a world with an extremely high division of labour. No modern economy can function without having at least some market segments. At the same time experience has shown that 'free' markets when left to themselves are often not a very satisfactory regulator of economic life. They produce results which are regarded as unacceptable for social and economic reasons. In real life therefore we meet only mixed economies where various forms of markets are combined with market regulations, policy interventions, public activities, institutional barriers, etc. These mixtures can assume a great variety of forms which reach from almost 'free' markets to extremely regulated systems.

In contrast to this reality of a range of mixed economies with different institutions and differing mechanisms, we have a traditional theoretical model which analyses the processes and mechanisms of a 'pure' and perfect market economy and take this model as a starting point for further investigations which can then allow for additional influences. This research strategy has enabled economists to reach highly sophisticated insights into the nature and effects of market mechanisms, but it has also created a tendency towards a somewhat dogmatic fixation on market processes which is intensified by seeing them in the idealized light of neoclassical models of general equilibrium. Markets have thus obtained a certain dominance in the realm of theory. Since in practice markets cannot exist in isolation, however, the question about the *actual* role of markets in the mixed economy – the question of 'how much market' is desirable – cannot be neglected. And since the answers to this question can have serious repercussions on various social and economic interests, it is not surprising that the problem of markets, of their role and their regulation, gives rise to heated discussions with considerable emotional undertones. The interest groups which benefit from market solutions then lend further support to the theoretical market bias. In this process 'the market' has increasingly tended to take on an ideological value of its own which is supported by economic (functional) and non-economic, partly ethical, arguments. A short survey of the main arguments involved are therefore in order when we consider ethical-economic points of contact.

Ever since Adam Smith right up to our day, the basic economic theory has shown a clear bias in favour of markets as a regulator of the economic process. Market mechanisms are not only analysed and explained, they are usually also recommended when a choice has to be made between alternative methods of regulation.[1] Two reasons are particularly responsible for this situation. The first has already been mentioned. The fact that economic theory has chosen perfect, well-functioning markets as a standard model from which reality might deviate but to which it can – hopefully! – be approximated has contributed to a strong positively oriented pro-market perspective. The undisputed capacity of perfect markets to adjust quickly and flexibly to changing circumstances is projected too uncritically to a real world which is pretty far removed from the perfect standards expected in the model. This bias is the more questionable since the 'theory of the second-best' shows that once some of the basic assumptions of a system are not met, it may be advantageous to change some of the rules which were regarded as optimal in the ideal setting. This means that in imperfect market environments, mere 'market conformity' might not be the best prescription for economic policy and might produce unexpected results.

The second reason for a positive valuation of (perfect) markets is derived from a positive valuation of the allocational effects produced by a market system. Assuming flexible processes, flexible prices, competition and high degrees of information and mobility, it can be shown that the market mechanism leads to a pattern of production which can be regarded as 'efficient' under the perspective of satisfying the final demands (backed by purchasing power) of a population. 'Efficiency' is here defined as Pareto-efficiency.[2] Questions and problems surrounding the idea of Pareto-efficiency will be treated in the following chapter. Here it is sufficient to point out that the idolization of the market system on the basis of its assumed or real efficiency characteristics implies a value judgement, namely the judgement that 'allocative efficiency' should be *the* decisive criterion in policy considerations even though the normal choice problem between different policy alternatives also involves a number of other economic and non-economic (social, political and ethical) targets. These may also be relevant and should be included in valuations and recommendations.

One could, of course, argue that this efficiency-based market bias could be seen as a purely economic 'technocratic' evaluation without any ethical connotations or consequences. But this view cannot be maintained. The decision for a comprehensive market solution also always includes a number of other consequences, among which questions of income distribution are particularly relevant, and certainly involves highly sensitive problems of ethics and justice (as we shall see in Chapter 9). Depending on the initial conditions (wealth, education, etc.) of market participants, market processes can lead to very different income distributions which may all be Pareto-efficient but may vary widely under considerations of justice (however defined). The 'purely' economic recommendation for the market can therefore only have limited relevance. Economists who recognize that the efficiency postulate cannot stand by itself as a comprehensive value principle argue that it should be supplemented or modified through a consideration of other values, in particular social and ethical ones. This can lead to modified policy recommendations which suggest interventions in the market process and/or changes in the initial conditions. Such reformist ideas still accept the market as an efficient standard, but point to a need for modifications. As examples of such views one can mention the models of a 'Soziale Marktwirtschaft' (social market economy, A. Müller-Armack), or of a socialist market economy (O. Lange).

A rather extreme economic point of view in favour of markets which used to be prominent 100 years ago but has lost importance since then defends markets, not only on allocational, but also on distributional and ethical grounds. Building on marginal utility and marginal productivity theory, market results are declared to be 'just' and 'morally right' because everybody is paid 'according to his [economic] contribution' and such a system of payment corresponds to moral principles.[3] Marginal productivity theory serves as a basis because it shows that in perfect competitive markets every factor of production would obtain in its own market (goods, labour, capital) a payment which corresponds exactly to its marginal product, the marginal product being that product which one unit of this factor (the 'last' or marginal unit) adds to total output.

Yet even if we were prepared to accept the assumption that real factor markets correspond to perfect markets – an assumption which is patently wrong! – such a moral justification of market results rests on very shaky foundations. Already the preliminary postulate that people's incomes and living conditions should be proportional to their economic performance is anything but a *self-evident* moral or just principle (as we shall see in Chapter 9). But we can let it pass as one possible principle among several which will appear plausible and acceptable to many persons. Particularly when we are faced with relatively simple and transparent conditions and similar starting points for all individuals, it can provide a useful 'ethical' standard. Take for instance a number of people who are given permission to gather apples in an orchard during one day. It is not difficult to regard as 'just' the proposal that at the end of the day everybody should be entitled to take home the apples which he himself has collected.

But the situation becomes far more problematic when we turn to a highly differentiated social economy. Quite apart from fundamental objections which point out the very unequal starting positions or the neglect of important non-market activities (domestic work, social services, etc.), the marginal product as such is not a suitable category for distributional judgements. Marginal products of capital, labour, raw materials and other inputs can serve as a basis for an efficient allocation of factors of production in different applications provided the technology permits sufficient substitution between factors. But the social output as a whole is the result of the common application of all factors. Neither is it possible to isolate the social contribution of one factor category alone; nor does the marginal product tell us anything about the 'effort' or 'sacrifice' of single factor units. Though in an extreme case the *marginal* product of labour may fall to zero in a given branch of the economy when the labour supply increases, it still remains true that the contribution of labour as a whole is positive and a *sine qua non* for obtaining any output. Moreover in the economy as a whole (as opposed to single branches) the concept of marginal productivity of generalized factors of production ('labour', 'capital', etc.) tends to become rather vague and abstract because of the extreme heterogeneity of the factors, the products and the technological processes used. If, on the other hand, distribution is based on the more concrete marginal products of individual branches, then incomes will no longer depend solely on the efforts a person undertakes to contribute to the common welfare (which could form an acceptable ethical criterion), but to a large extent on exogenous influences such as the quantity of the factor under consideration, the quantity of complementary factors, the development of technological and demand conditions, etc. Although these influences are relevant as indicators for efficient reallocations of factors of production, the income patterns they produce have little to do with personal endeavours and distributional justice. And last but not least the pertinent question remains whether incomes from the factor capital, such as incomes from (partly inherited) wealth, should – from a moral point of view – be regarded as equivalent to incomes from personal effort.

The idealizations of the market mentioned so far are all connected more or less directly with standard economic theory, with its efficiency and distributional aspects. But there are also other authors presenting the market as a positive value in itself who do not base their arguments on the instrumental qualities of markets but start directly from political-ethical premises. A prominent position in this camp is held by representatives of classical liberalism. Economists like F. von Hayek and M. Friedman, the 'Chicago School' and others regard the market not only as an instrument for economic efficiency, but also as a political-moral institution for the maintenance of individual freedom. Freedom of personal choice and freedom of contracts in competitive markets are meant to protect the individual from undue regulation or interference from the government and other public authorities. 'Free markets', 'deregulation' and 'privatization' become in this perspective absolute norms which are not derived (solely) from their economic usefulness, but are ethical demands in the interests of individual freedom.

It can easily be seen that this advocacy of the market as

a 'moral institution' rests on the old liberal idea of 'freedom *from* the state'. But it does not deal with the problem of 'freedom *in* the state'. Or in other words, if we distinguish between passive and active freedom (where the first refers to freedom from interference by third persons while the second deals with the opportunities for achieving one's aims), then we can say that the market postulate of the liberals is restricted to the problem of passive freedom. One of the problems of markets in general and of monopolistic and oligopolistic markets in particular is, however, that they lead to very uneven distributions of active freedom both in economic and in non-economic spheres (since money is a basis for power). If active freedom is to be included in the ethical 'portfolio' then market dogma and the maxim of non-interventionism of the liberal school lose their moral credentials.

Of a quite different nature is a philosophical defence of unrestricted markets on conservative juridical-ethical grounds advanced by R. Nozick. In his approach, economic arguments become completely irrelevant. The unfettered market with all its effects – be they desirable or undesirable – is to be morally accepted because it represents the historical development of a framework in which 'entitlements' (property and transaction rights) are lawfully acquired and transmitted. Preservation of rights is seen as the highest moral principle which must not be disturbed by any interference into market processes where such entitlements are acquired and exchanged. Here obvious ethical problems arise with regard to the absolute nature of the rule that rights are supreme without regard to any 'losses' or disadvantages which its application may produce. This is a complete negation of consequential ethics. In the context of free market operations it means that the drug trade, starvation wages, even the sale of oneself into slavery all become ethically irrelevant or at least are not allowed to encourage market interference. This is a principle which comes into conflict with quite a number of competing ethical systems.

In contrast to the views propounding the virtues of markets which we have discussed so far, there are others which take a more disillusioned or critical view of the market as a dominant institution. Approaches which start from a closer observation of real markets than from an idealized market model are generally concerned with their actual performance and their qualities in relation to various economic desiderata like allocational efficiency, economic growth, stability and distribution. In this perspective 'free' markets appear as an institution which in many respects can serve as a useful instrument, but which at the same time is open to disturbances with serious negative effects. Depending on the situation and the problem, more or less market, more or less intervention, may seem advisable. The market loses its special priority position. Keynesian, institutional and radical theories tend to view the market from such a perspective.

Even further removed from market advocates than these 'illusion-free' approaches are critical views which adopt a hostile attitude to the market as a dominant system on moral grounds of a different vintage. Three variants of such views can serve as examples. The first one is as old as the capitalist market economy and rests on a moral rejection of the wide income differences which the market produces. This leads to a demand for intervention which will – *ex ante* or *ex post* – correct these distributional tendencies. A more fundamental criticism which condemns competitive markets as such deplores the fact that competition, the drive for profits and personal advantage destroy valuable ethical human qualities like sympathy, solidarity and compassion. Alternative social and economic relations are desired even if this causes a certain loss in 'efficiency'. And finally we find more recent scepticism concerning unrestricted market mechanisms in connection with a greater awareness of the growing ecological and generational problematique. This awareness, which partly rests on ethical roots, warns that the failure of markets to give sufficient weight to external effects represents a growing danger in a world of dwindling resources and accelerating technological uncertainties. These problems should get higher priority in place of the traditional belief in the equilibrating and corrective forces of free markets.

Notes

1. The contemporary debates about ecological problems show this very clearly. When for instance questions of air pollution are discussed, it is conspicuous how economists tend to prefer marketable 'pollution certificates' to other solutions (e.g. general limits, prohibitions, etc.) without giving much thought to the socio-political and institutional framework and the way it may influence the enforcement and effectiveness of various measures.
2. Pareto-efficiency is a state of affairs where it is impossible to improve the (economic) position of any individual without causing a deterioration in the position of some other individual.
3. J. B. Clark's *The Distribution of Wealth* (1899) was an outstanding example of this line of reasoning.

6. Welfare Economics

The decision to become an economic theorist can originate from different motives. Leaving aside the cases where chance was at work or where this activity was chosen as one of many equally attractive career opportunities, we are left with two important motives. One may be attracted to a theoretical study of economic processes on 'purely' scientific grounds in order to throw light on the complex relationships in this sphere. Or the impulse may come from a social motivation to improve the economic lot of some or possibly all persons. Theoretical work is then seen as a contribution to our capacity to shape economic processes for social ends.

These two motives are not mutually exclusive and may both be at work in one and the same person. Since both refer to the same object – the economy – they also overlap in their theoretical analysis. Differences appear when it comes to questions posed and problems treated and are also reflected in the form in which research results are presented. Where 'pure scientific' interests prevail, the theoretical work will tend to be concentrated on complex mechanisms and relationships and the results will normally be presented free from any emotions and valuations. This approach comes nearest to the strict postulates of 'Wertfreiheit' which we discussed earlier. Where social motivation is the driving force, the centre of interest normally lies in a socio-economically relevant problem (economic growth, poverty, etc.) which is analysed with the intention of finding a 'solution' to the problem. Valuations and recommendations for 'improvements' are typical in these approaches. As we have argued in Chapter 3, this need not be regarded as a violation of scientific principles as long as the chosen values are openly declared and are not permitted to falsify the analytical framework. But the fact remains that in this second ('social') case, open or hidden ethical elements and valuations will normally play a bigger role than in 'purely scientific' approaches.

On the whole it is true to say that in the course of time economists and economic theories have *in principle* shown a strong tendency in favour of a 'scientific-positive' analysis, with valuations and normative statements being banished and relegated to special branches like 'applied economics' or 'economic policy'. While throughout the 19th century it was still a fairly universal practice to include and mix ethical and factual considerations in theoretical studies, the 20th century and particularly the inter-war period saw the rise of a changed attitude which advocated a sharper division between positive 'scientific' theory on the one hand and normative statements on the other.

Yet notwithstanding this new methodological outlook, the fundamental motive to give economic advice not just as an ordinary citizen but also and particularly as an economic expert could not so easily be deflected. That such a coexistence of theory and recommendations can be accepted practice would seem to be proved by medical research or in the work of engineers. Doctors have no inhibitions whatsoever in investigating the toxic characteristics of a foodstuff and insisting at the same time that its sale should be prohibited. Similarly, an engineer who has constructed a new machine will not hesitate to recommend its use because of its greater efficiency. But the value judgements involved in these cases have one important quality: they rest on valuations which are supported by a very broad social consensus. That health is preferable to illness and that productive efficiency should be increased are ideas so widely accepted that their combination with theoretical statements hardly creates any problems.

In the case of macroeconomics and other social sciences,

we are normally faced with a more complicated situation. Valuations and recommendations, whether connected with theoretical ideas or not, usually lead to a complex system of results which can affect the interests of different persons and groups in very different ways. There are no such simple and clear targets like 'health' which can command general acceptance. This applies also to the value which is so near to the heart of economists – 'allocative efficiency' – which is a *partial* target competing with other values, in particular with distribution problems. Normative statements in economics therefore do not only involve ethical and other value systems; they are necessarily burdened with conflicts between values and aims. Normative statements in social science are therefore not as 'innocent' as those in medical examples. They require a sceptical investigation with regard to their explicit or implicit ethical assumptions.

The conflict between the wish to overcome theoretical sterility and to give 'theoretically grounded' advice on the one hand and the fact that there cannot be any simple, unequivocal link between theoretical results and policy recommendations on the other has given rise to a special branch of economic theory – welfare economics – which tries to overcome this conflict. The development of welfare economics offers an instructive picture of the aforementioned tendency towards a stricter 'scientification' of economic theory, towards a clearer segregation of 'is' and 'ought' statements.

The development of welfare economics can be divided into two clearly distinguishable phases: those of 'Old Welfare Economics' and 'New Welfare Economics', with the late 1930s as the dividing line. Though we shall be mainly concerned with the New Welfare Economics in this chapter, both because it is the ruling version and because in it the theory-ethics dilemma is particularly visible, we shall first say a few words about the older version. This is useful partly because the problems and traditions of the Old Welfare Economics are still present and valid, and partly because looking at the past will help us to bring the ideas and problems of the New Welfare Economics more clearly into focus.

The Old Welfare Economics, which reached its climax in A. Pigou's grand opus *The Economics of Welfare* (1920), developed round about the turn of the century. This was a time when tendencies were growing to get away from the rather naive mixture of positive and normative elements in economic theory which had been the rule in the work of the classics. Welfare economics had its roots in the desire of many economists to maintain contact between theoretical analysis and socially relevant themes. The task of economic studies should certainly be to explain and analyse economic relationships, but this should also be done with an eye on questions of general material welfare and a growth of 'general utility'. This perspective influenced the structure of the analysis (production-distribution-consumption) and then led quite naturally to more far-reaching considerations in which theoretical insights were discussed in the light of their relevance and usefulness as contributions to general welfare. A welfare economics was born.

A typical characteristic of the Old Welfare Economics was the ethical belief that higher material welfare and particularly a better provision of essential goods are desirable targets, even though it was usually acknowledged that material welfare and utility cannot be equated with general welfare or 'happiness'. Analytical and empirical studies relevant to such a perspective were regarded as particularly important. It was regarded as desirable that the usual scientific methods (analysis, empirical studies, etc.) should be fully mobilized in the treatment of these subjects. But when these methods were not applicable to some urgent questions, one should not hesitate to supplement them with 'softer' considerations like plausibility, common sense or introspection in order to keep in touch with the welfare problem.

In following such a strategy the Old Welfare Economics

was prepared to work with rather simple and robust assumptions about utility and utility effects so as to be able to come to realistic welfare statements. Though aware that no simple objective method existed to compare the subjective utility levels of different persons, one did not hesitate to make assumptions about relative utility gains and losses in connection with alternative policy proposals. This was made easier and more plausible because such comparisons of utility did not normally refer to single individuals but to *groups* of persons (such as rich and poor) where one could assume that *on average* significant and typical differences existed. This reasoning was further supported by the generally accepted economic 'law' of diminishing marginal utility (for goods and money) which was regarded as valid for all individuals. On the basis of such considerations – ethical, psychological and economic – it was not a big step to recommend, for instance, a certain income transfer from the rich to the poor. In terms of utilitarian ideas this would lead to an increase in the 'sum of utilities'. In the case where a higher living standard also improved the productivity of the poor, even total output could rise leading to further general utility effects.

The 'scenario' of the previous paragraph is merely meant to indicate the motivations and research strategies of the Old Welfare Economics. Its approach found a reflection in many themes and played a pioneering role in some other fields (external effects, market failure). There is no need to go into these ramifications here. The important point to note is the general approach of the Old Welfare Economics which was characterized by a combination of an ethical commitment *vis-à-vis* improvements in material welfare with solid theoretical analysis, supplemented – where necessary – by 'robust' general observations and assumptions[1] in order to arrive at a basis for realistic and (in principle) realizable recommendations and policies.

For more than 50 years now this earlier phase has been replaced by New Welfare Economics as the ruling paradigm. Born from a strengthened trend for a clearer 'scientific' delineation of economic theory and from a changed emphasis in defining economics, welfare economics took on a very different appearance. The change in accent had already begun in the 1870s with the triumphant advance of marginal utility theories when interest switched increasingly from the 'wealth of nations' (Adam Smith), with its emphasis on the social division of labour and the exchange of goods as sources of material plenty, to an investigation of individual choice and action in the market. Individual utility in production and consumption and its satisfaction as a driving force for action (which is constrained by a scarcity of resources) became the central problem in economic theory; at the same time, the investigation of 'allocative efficiency' as a choice process became a decisive research subject. This change in emphasis found clear expression in Lionel Robbins's famous and widely-used definition of 1932 that 'economics is the science which studies human behaviour as a relationship between ends and scarce means which have alternative uses'.[2]

Behind this change, however, the old utilitarian tradition remained alive insofar as most economists still adhere – explicitly or implicitly – to the idea that increases in utility or utility maximization are desirable aims. But the perspective has shifted from some general utility for society as a whole to the separate utilities of single individuals which cannot be aggregated into a societal sum-total. This individualized perspective, which corresponds to the methodological individualism of the new 'subjective' theories, was fortified by a positivistic methodology which stressed the impossibility of obtaining reliable observations for utility levels and interpersonal comparisons of utility. Statements on total utility and similar matters should therefore be avoided in scientific research since they are bare of 'scientific content'.

Thus, the Old Welfare Economics was dethroned. But the old dilemma of economists persisted; they still wanted and still want to be able to give 'theoretically valid' advice which is not just an expression of their personal value preferences (which they are 'permitted' to promote in non-scientific conversation). It was this dilemma and the attempt to overcome it which prepared the ground for the New Welfare Economics whose principles were laid down about 1940 by John Hicks, Nicholas Kaldor and Tibor Scitovsky. It will be obvious that the task of building a bridge between a narrowly-defined notion of science and science-based normative statements would not be an easy one. And in fact, as we shall see, it could only be achieved by some ingenious and to some extent questionable 'tricks'.

This brings us now to a more detailed treatment of the New Welfare Economics or simply 'welfare economics' in what follows. This subject, with its problem of bridging the gap between a positive economic theory and normative statements, belongs – together with income distribution problems (Chapter 9) – at the core of the theory-ethics complex.

Two elements occupy a central place in modern welfare economics: the notion of Pareto-optimality and the role of perfect markets in connection with Pareto-optimality. Building on these elements, a superstructure of further ideas and results can be erected which keeps the welfare-theoretical discussion going. The notion of the Pareto-optimum – named after earlier ideas of the Italian economist and sociologist Vilfredo Pareto – has gained importance because it opens an escape (though a narrow one!) from the difficulty of evaluating and comparing macro-situations on a utility principle even when interpersonal utility comparisons are not admitted. While the Old Welfare Economics had no difficulty in stating that situation *Y* was 'better' than situation *X* because the utility gains of the winners from a change to *Y* were 'obviously' greater than the utility losses of the losers, this argumentation was closed to the New Welfare economists. Interpersonal utility comparisons were now regarded as impossible and meaningless. A change in a multi-person situation should only be regarded as an unequivocal improvement if some people were better off in the new situation and no person worse off than before. This is the basic idea of Pareto.

If a situation *Y* represents such an improvement in comparison with situation *X*, then we say that *Y* is pareto-superior to *X*, and *X* pareto-inferior to *Y*. If for instance I prefer apples to oranges but have only oranges in my possession while somebody else prefers oranges but possesses apples, then a change of apples against oranges will obviously lead to a pareto-superior situation: both of us will be better off. But if I just take the other person's apples, this cannot be regarded as an 'improvement' even if these apples save me from starvation and the other person is only slightly irritated by the loss of some apples. Pareto-*optimality* is then a situation where no further opportunity exists to find a pareto-superior solution; in other words the lot of no person can then be improved without reducing somebody else's utility.

A noteworthy and in theory not unimportant characteristic of Pareto-optimality is that there exists a close relationship between this notion and the theoretical model of 'free' and perfect markets. This can be illustrated in a simplified way by looking at the exchange of (two) goods between two persons with the aid of a so-called Edgeworth-Box. In Figure 6.1 we have a 'Box' where quantities of the good *X* can be read off in horizontal directions and quantities of good *Y* in vertical directions. The quantities of *X* and *Y* are given and equal to the dimensions of the box. Each point within the box depicts a certain distribution of *X* and *Y* between two persons *A* and *B*, with the quantities belonging to *A* measured from point *A* and those belonging to *B* measured from point *B*. Thus the point *a* refers to a situation where *A* possesses the combination AX_A of *X* and AY_A of *Y* and *B* is consequently in control of BX_B and BY_B. The curves within the box represent a few of *A*'s and *B*'s indifference curves indicating

Figure 6.1 Edgworth Box and Pareto-optimality

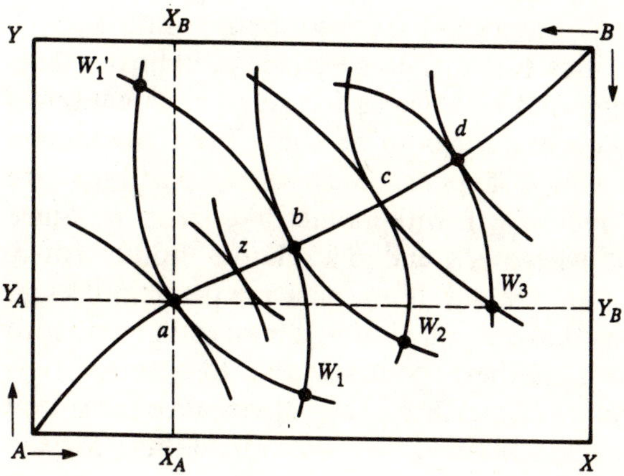

their preferences for different combinations of X and Y. The curves which are convex from below (seen from point A) are the indifference curves of A and conversely for B. The greater the distance from A (or B), the greater the amount of goods and the utility of the person concerned.

We start with an initial situation where the distribution of the goods X and Y between A and B is given by W_1. As the slope of an indifference curve indicates the relative marginal utilities of the two goods, we see that in W_1 the relative utilities of X and Y are not the same for A and B. A is prepared to give up quite a number of X units for additional Y without loss of utility, while the converse is true for B. If 'free' exchange prevails (with nobody forced to exchange and nobody prevented from it), then both A and B will find it advantageous to exchange goods. Starting from W_1 A will transfer X to B and obtain Y. In this way they will move to distribution situations which lie between the two indifference curves W_1 W_1' passing through point

W_1. In this area both *A* and *B* are on a higher indifference curve than in W_1, therefore their utility increases. W_1 is thus clearly pareto-inferior to these alternative positions: free exchange (free markets) leads to 'better' situations.

The opportunities for further pareto-type improvements through exchange end as soon as the relative valuation of *X* versus *Y* is the same for both persons. Then any motive for exchange will disappear. Such final positions are exemplified in Figure 6.1 with points like *a*, *z*, *b*. Since these are points where *A*'s and *B*'s relative utilities for *X* and *Y* are the same, the indifference curves passing through these points must have equal slopes: they are tangential to each other. Each of these points is Pareto-optimal; it is easy to see that a departure from them favouring one person can only be obtained at a cost (in utility) for the other person. This is, of course, the reason why an exchange favouring both parties is no longer possible. Since in a general equilibrium of perfect markets (with complete market clearing), the relative marginal utilities for all market participants and over the whole range of goods are the same (which causes exchange acts to come to a rest in the equilibrium position), we can conclude that (perfect) market equilibria are Pareto-optimal. This does not only apply to a pure exchange model, but also to models including production as long as the strict assumptions of perfect markets (perfect competition, flexibility, information) are extended from the goods markets to the factor markets.

Let us return to Figure 6.1. When we draw a line through all the tangency-points of *A*'s and *B*'s indifference curves (*a*, *b*, *c*, *d* . . . *z*) we obtain the curve *AB* which is called the 'contract curve'. It is the locus of all possible Pareto-optimal distributions of the given amounts of *X* and *Y*. Every other distribution is pareto-inferior insofar as it permits 'improvements' (through free exchange or otherwise) which will benefit both persons. But no valuation or ordering is possible *between* points on the contract curve as long as interpersonal comparisons of utility are not permitted.

There is no room for setting the gains of one person against the losses of the other in order to reach an aggregate net balance. Even points like *A* and *B*, where one of the persons has all the goods, are Pareto-optimal because handing over some of the goods to the other person would lead to a deterioration of the possessor's position.

Although each point (each constellation) on the contract curve is Pareto-optimal and can be the result of some exchange process, the collection of points that can be reached in a concrete situation is limited and depends on initial conditions. In our example of Figure 6.1, initial conditions are given by the amounts of *X* and *Y* which *A* and *B* own before exchange takes place. If these are given by W_1 then the (pareto-superior) exchange result must lie between *a* and *b*. In *a* *A* would be just as well off as before, but *B* would be far better off; in *b* the situation would be the other way round. In between these two situations all points on the contract curve would yield utility gains for both partners. Combinations to the south–west of *a* or to the north–east of *b* are irrelevant because in these situations one of the partners would be worse off than in W_1 and would therefore refuse to enter into such a transaction. The range *a–b* is called the 'core' of the 'solution' for W_1 as the initial condition; it covers all possible Pareto-optimal positions which can be reached in a process of free exchange.[3] In an analogous way we obtain as core for W_2 the range *b–c*, for W_3 *c–d* and so on.

The connection between initial conditions and core can be pictured more directly with the aid of a utility possibility curve as given in Figure 6.2 (where we assume that the utility levels of the two persons *A* and *B* can be presented by indices which, however, need not be comparable). The axes in the diagram 6.2 contain the utility scale of *A* (U_A) and of *B* (U_B) respectively. The curve connecting the two axes contains all the utility combinations of *A* and *B* along the contract curve of Figure 6.1. The highest point of the possibility curve on the ordinate corresponds to the situ-

Figure 6.2 Utility possibility curve

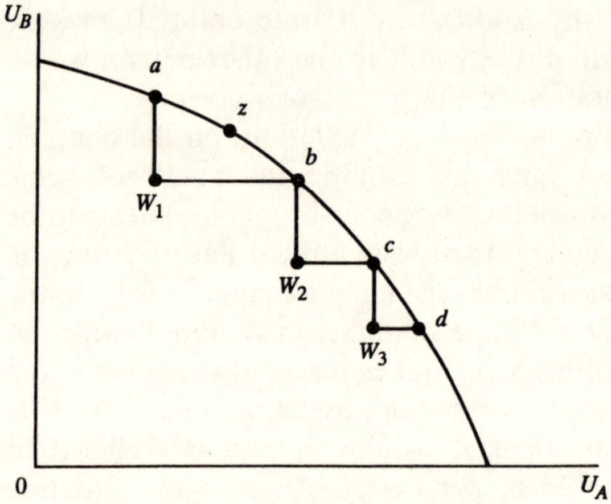

ation where *B* obtains all the goods and *A* nothing. Consequently *B* reaches his maximum possible utility while *A*'s utility is zero. Other distributions of *X* and *Y* lead to different (shared) utility combinations. The negative slope of the curve expresses Pareto-optimality; in each situation an increase in the utility of one person can only be achieved at the cost of a utility loss of the other. The concavity of the curve (*vis-à-vis* the origin) takes account of the assumption of diminishing marginal utility. Points above the possibility curve cannot be reached because the amounts of *X* and *Y* are limited; points below the curve represent pareto-inferior positions which can be rectified through exchange.

As before, we denote alternative initial conditions with W_1, W_2 and W_3. It can easily be seen that from each of these points only a limited number of positions on the possibility curve can be reached as 'core' solutions where no person would suffer a loss of utility. Thus, as in Figure 6.1, the core for W_1 is limited to the range *a–b*. Exactly where within this range the exchange process will ultimately arrive (i.e. how the utility gains will be distributed between *A* and *B*) cannot be determined in this two-person example. It will depend on the bargaining skills and strategies of the two partners and on chance influences. It can be shown, however, that with a growing number of market participants the core (for a given initial position) gets narrower and narrower until it is reduced to a single position on the possibility curve when the number of persons becomes very large. This is the position of the Pareto-optimal perfect market equilibrium.

This simplified model, which can be expanded to a comprehensive system of (perfect) competitive markets (with production, exchange and money), provides the basis for two fundamental theorems of welfare economics which lead to a normative bias in favour of market solutions. The first theorem ('direct theorem') tells us that under the assumption that individuals aim at utility maximization, free exchange (in perfect markets) will guarantee that a Pareto-optimal situation on the possibility curve (contract curve) will be reached. This we have already shown. The second theorem ('converse theorem') points out that every specific pareto-optimal position on the possibility (contract) curve is – in the case of atomistic competition – uniquely bound up with a certain initial condition. Thus with W_1 as an initial condition and large numbers of market participants, only one equilibrium condition would be reached, say z in Figures 6.1 and 6.2; conversely, z can be reached exactly by making W_1 the starting point for the exchange process.

Thus, starting from a rather simple basis, we have already obtained two rudimentary 'theoretically founded' normative welfare economic statements: (1) the 'scientific' denial that interpersonal comparisons of utility are possible and (2) the partly psychological, partly 'ethical' idea that additional material wealth will increase individual utility and that increases in utility are a desirable target. These stipulations, connected with the basic assumptions of general equilibrium theories, provide the basis for a normative pro-market stance. Though this framework does not permit an 'objective' decision as to *which* of the many Pareto-optimal situations deserves priority (since this would require interpersonal utility comparisons), it can still be said that 'free' competitive markets are a precondition for an optimal solution. Whatever concrete solution is desired – chosen under various political and ethical aspects – it should correspond to *some* market equilibrium. All other situations ought to be rejected because they are not Pareto-optimal.

If a particular Pareto-optimal situation is selected (for whatever reasons) as the desired target, it can be reached in two different ways. Let us assume that under the conditions depicted in Figures 6.1 and 6.2 a consensus exists that the position z is a desirable distribution. Let the initial (pareto-inferior) position be given by W_2. The distribution z does not belong to the core of W_2. To get to z one can use one of two possible paths. Either one permits the market (exchange) process to move from W_2 to a point within the W_2 core (i.e. from b to c) and then gets to z via a redistribution policy; or one starts off with an adjustment of initial conditions, substituting W_1 for W_2 and then lets the market move to z which is the core corresponding to W_1, assuming there are many market participants. The first strategy mirrors the 'direct theorem'; the second the 'converse theorem'.

Though these rudimentary 'theoretical' rules of welfare economics concerning competitive markets are plausible and can indeed be helpful on an abstract analytical plane, they become questionable as instruments as soon as we leave the idealized assumptions of general equilibrium models, as we must when we are concerned with recommendations for the *real* world. In this case we have to look at them more critically. In doing this we shall for the moment continue to accept the – by no means self-evident – normative background that an increase in individual utility levels of market participants (without interpersonal comparisons) is a sufficient ethical basis for (economic) priorities and recommendations. Aspects of this question will be taken up later on.

The close link between welfare economic aspirations and the characteristics of 'free markets' rests decisively on the elements ascribed to the 'perfect market' model. It begins to lose force and credibility as soon as the discrepancies between real markets and the model are taken into account. To ensure that all the processes and results under real conditions conform approximately to those of the model, it would first of all be necessary that most or all production and consumption transactions take place on markets characterized by a high degree of competition and information. But historical, institutional and practical influences are responsible for considerable deviations from such a situation. This is most clearly though by no means exclusively demonstrated on the 'labour market' with its enormous heterogeneity and institutional peculiarities. As soon as considerable sectors of the economy do not conform – even approximately – to the assumptions of equilibrium models of the neoclassical type, however, it is no longer guaranteed that the market recommendation will always lead to Pareto-optimal solutions. On the contrary, it may be necessary to use regulations, interventions or countervailing power in order to move nearer to Pareto-optimal situations.

To this fundamental objection further limitations to the 'market rule' can be added. The market bias of welfare economics stresses the importance of market equilibrium as an *essential precondition* for access to the spectre of Pareto-optimal constellations from which the ethical-political desired 'solution' can then be chosen and finally reached through redistribution or a rearrangement of initial conditions. But in relation to practical affairs, this perspective overlooks the fact that not only market processes but political and sociological processes as well are subjected to certain 'laws' which cannot be manipulated *ad libitum*. Redistributions of income and, even more, readjustments of initial conditions (wealth, access to education, etc.) are costly and meet with considerable economic and political resistance which cannot always be overcome. Different economic strategies will affect different interests and power positions and will influence the framework within which political action can become effective. Initial and market conditions by themselves cannot be linked directly and uniquely with specific final results. These will also depend on the instruments which are available and can be used to obtain readjustments; they are 'path-dependent'.

Consequences of these considerations for the argumentation of welfare economics can be illustrated with the aid of our simple model. In Figure 6.3 the continuous curve again represents all the possible Pareto-optimal utility combinations of *A* and *B* corresponding to various market

Figure 6.3 The utility possibility curve and the utility feasibility curve

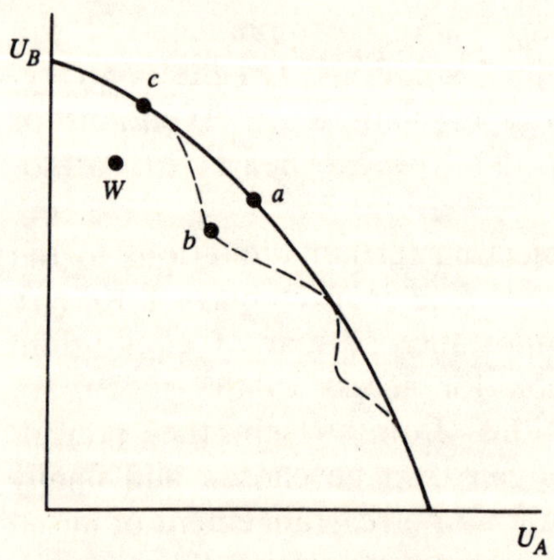

equilibria. But as a consequence of such factors as market imperfections, market failures and political barriers, not all of these constellations may be attainable. In addition to the utility possibility curve which could be reached under 'ideal' conditions, we get a second set of constellations which can actually be reached. They are shown (in 6.3) by the dotted curve, which can be called a 'utility feasibility frontier'.[4] The feasibility curve can coincide with the possibility curve but can also lie below it. Thus institutional or market restrictions may prevent a movement from *b* to *a* because of credit restrictions, price rigidities, etc. Let us now assume that we have initial conditions *W* and that a desired final distribution would be represented by *a*. An 'orthodox' recommendation would be to move through free exchange (markets) from *W* to *c* (the corresponding market equilibrium) and then move to *a* via a redistribution of incomes. But it may turn out that such a redistribution is politically not possible or too costly. It might, however, be possible to rearrange matters so that one gets from *W* directly to *b*. Since *b* lies on the feasibility frontier this is a terminal point; there is no path to the possibility curve. Thus we are faced with a situation that, starting from *W*, a market process would result in a Pareto-optimal equilibrium (*c*). However, it may be preferable to move to the sub-optimal feasible situation *b* which – though sub-optimal *vis-à-vis* the unattainable optimum *a* – may be preferred to *c*. The rule that *every* desired utilitarian solution must always and necessarily also be a Pareto-optimal market equilibrium loses its simple force once the influence of real world complexities are taken into account.

After these remarks, which should prevent us from accepting too uncritically pro-market norms purely on the basis of welfare economic arguments, we can now turn to other and more specific aspects of the New Welfare Economics. In doing this we continue to adhere to the basic principles of welfare economics – the utilitarian idea of 'more is better' and the pareto-optimum as a standard in view of the negation of interpersonal comparisons of utility. But we need no longer feel bound to assume perfect markets or any other market hypothesis.

One of the main weaknesses of a welfare economics whose ultimate aim is to be able to produce usable recommendations for economic policy is the fact that one can usually reject a number of constellations quite easily because of their pareto-inferiority, but that the Pareto-principle does not offer any criterion as to which of the several possible Pareto-optimal situations should be preferred. This problem of finding an 'optimum optimorum', a 'best' Pareto-optimal situation, did not exist for the Old Welfare Economics. There it was permitted to compare the probable utilities to be gained or lost by different groups in different optimal situations and then to choose the one which promised to deliver the highest aggregate utility. This path was closed to the New Welfare economists who rejected the comparison or summation of utilities. A way out of this difficulty was needed and towards the end of the 1930s two alternative 'solutions' were developed. One was proposed by Abram Bergson[5] who suggested the construction of a determinate and unique social preference function to be derived from all individual preferences which would allow a generally acceptable ordering of different pareto-optimal constellations to obtain. Figure 6.4 is an illustration of Bergson's idea. As before the diagram contains the utility combinations of *A* and *B*. The curve *VV* represents all Pareto-optimal situations which can be effectively obtained. The *WW'* curves are part of the social preference or welfare function. Each *WW'* curve contains constellations which are equally acceptable to the community, curves higher up indicating a higher preference. In the diagram the position *P*, where a social indifference curve touches the utility possibility curve *VV*, is the 'optimum optimorum': it is the Pareto-optimal position which yields the highest possible socially accepted satisfaction.

In theory (disregarding practical difficulties in appli-

Figure 6.4 A social preference function

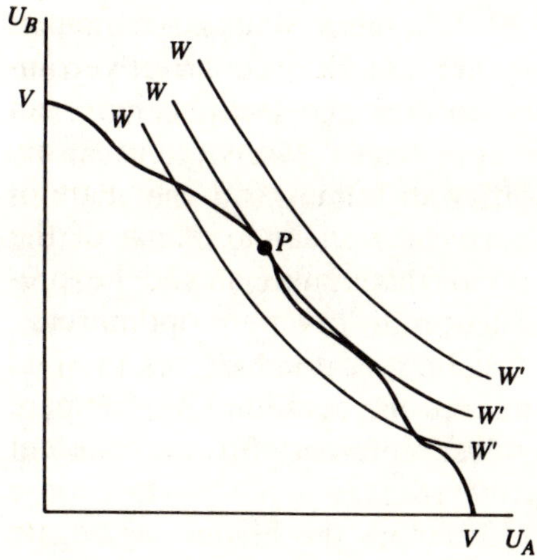

cation), Bergson's method would seem to offer a satisfactory compromise for deriving more definite decisions within the chosen 'scientific-normative' framework of welfare economics. But his proposal is undermined by weaknesses in the concept of a social preference function. Since with other economists Bergson rejects the possibility of adding up individual utilities in order to obtain aggregate utilities, some other method has to be found which would allow such an aggregate social function to be constructed which could take account of all individual preferences. Yet Kenneth Arrow has shown in his famous 'impossibility theorem' that – given some plausible minimal requirements regarding consistency and correspondence with individual preferences – no definite and unique social preference function can be derived except under very special conditions (such as when all individual preference functions are identical).[6] Of course, this does not mean that in practice it might not be possible to arrive at a social consensus in policy matters. Discussions, institutional arrangements and judicial processes can all help to approach 'solutions' which are more or less generally acceptable and can serve as a basis for decision-making. But these solutions are the result of a political process and are not derived directly from individual preferences, nor do they necessarily correspond to all the individual preference scales. Moreover it can be shown that results will differ depending on the method used to reach a consensus (see the example of the voting paradox in the Appendix to this chapter): there is no guarantee of unique, consistent or even Pareto-optimal outcomes. Ethical considerations, political influence and institutional constraints all influence the decision process. This is not the same thing as a social preference function derived directly from individual preferences.

The second attempt to overcome the limitations of the New Welfare Economics without endangering its basic assumptions appeared one year after Bergson's proposal in two papers by Kaldor and Hicks.[7] Since the main weakness of the New Welfare Economics was that it permitted recommendations only in cases where no person would be harmed – a constellation which is rather exceptional in practice – Kaldor and Hicks proposed an extension of the welfare criterion. It should be applicable to all situations in which a pareto-superior improvement could be achieved *in principle* even if not executed in practice. Accordingly a situation *Y* is to be regarded as 'better' than *X* even when some persons in *Y* are worse off than before as long as the gains of the winning groups are big enough to compensate fully all the losers and still leave some surplus to the winners. If the compensation actually takes place, a pareto-type improvement has obviously been achieved: the losers are now not worse off than before and the others have reached a higher level of utility.

With this extension, welfare economics is obviously given a much wider scope for practical relevance. Its normative recommendations are now no longer restricted to situations which yield a general improvement *directly* for all persons; it suffices that room for *potential* general improvement is created. On this basis one could hope to march from pareto-inferior to (potentially) pareto-superior situations, thus gradually approaching an 'optimal' Pareto-optimum. Unfortunately there are two flaws in this 'solution': a very serious one on the practical (applied) side and a formal one which is of more theoretical interest.

The practical difficulty is connected with the notion of *potential* improvements through compensation. From the point of view of a theory-oriented welfare economics, this device has its attractions. It opens the chance that 'on a purely theoretical basis' one can point out where (pareto-type) improvements are possible and therefore *in principle commendable* but leave it to the political process to carry out (or not) the potentially possible compensation. Since such compensation is often not undertaken and since the political possibilities of achieving it are not totally independent from chosen economic policies, it becomes doubtful whether the compensation principle in this form of an *abstract possibility* is really a great step forward in making 'pure' welfare economics more relevant in terms of realistic scenarios. Under this principle it could be possible to step continually from one 'improvement' to another, but with some sections of the population becoming continuously poorer because the potential compensations did not actually take place. Because of this some economists (such as Pareto and Little) have suggested – in contrast to Kaldor – that a change should be called an 'improvement' only if the compensations safeguarding the Pareto-principle are actually paid. But if this restriction is adopted we are back where we were before. Welfare economics will again not be able to pass any judgement in most practical situations because full and comprehensive compensation is an exception rather than a rule in a complex world with a very uneven distribution of power and influence.

A formal difficulty connected with the compensation

principle was brought up in a paper by Scitovsky[8] who pointed out that, quite apart from the practical question raised in the previous paragraph, in some circumstances the Kaldor solution cannot deliver a clear decision. The essence of Scitovsky's argument can be presented in the following simplified form. Let us deal with a situation where new technological or institutional conditions permit a shift in the utility possibility curve: the question arises whether a possible change should be carried out. In the terms of welfare economics the question is whether the (market-determined) pareto-optimum under the changed circumstances is pareto-superior to the Pareto-optimum in present circumstances, in which case the change should be 'recommended'. If this is not the case, it should be 'rejected'.

We start off with a situation where the Kaldor-principle does not cause any problems. In Figure 6.5 we have a utility possibility curve U_1U_1' in the initial situation which

Figure 6.5 The compensation principle

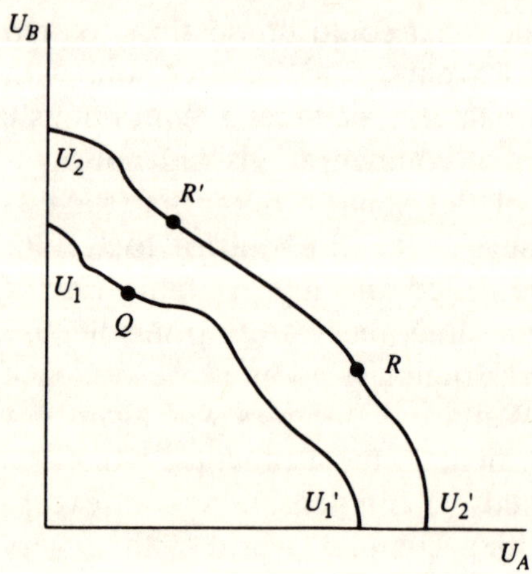

could be shifted – through new economic arrangements – to $U_2U'_2$. In the initial condition we have an equilibrium in Q; after the change a new equilibrium would be established (through the market or otherwise) in R. Both positions are Pareto-optimal. The question is: is R preferable to Q and should the change be effected? According to the compensation principle the answer is quite clearly 'yes'. It is true that the actual change will cause a loss of utility for B, but a potential redistribution (compensation) could shift the situation from R to R' which represents an improvement for both persons.

Let us now assume a situation as given in Figure 6.6. As before $U_1U'_1$ and Q represent the initial condition, and $U_2U'_2$ are the new possibilities under discussion. A changeover to the new situation would result in R. As before we could regard this as an improvement since A could compensate B in such a way that R' is reached where both A and B are better off than in Q. But once the change to

Figure 6.6 Compensation and the Scitovsky problem

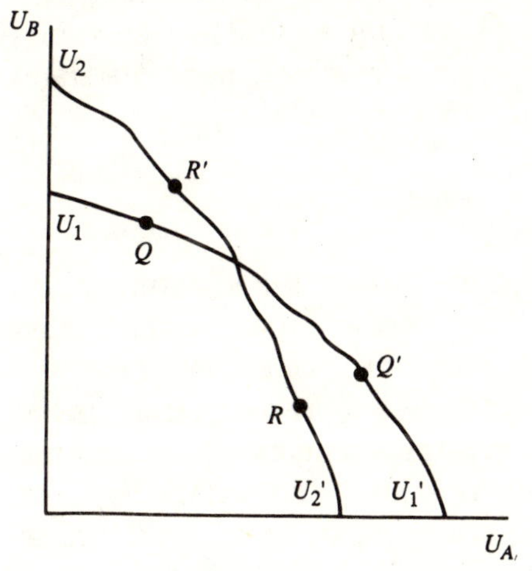

R has taken place it can be seen that, *from this perspective*, Q is now preferable to R. For if we change 'back' (from U_2U_2' to U_1U_1') A will at first be disadvantaged. But through compensation from B to A we can move from Q to Q' where both A and B are better off than in R. Thus depending on the situation from which we start, a different Pareto-optimal situation will appear as preferable. No unequivocal result emerges.[9]

We can conclude that the ambition of the New Welfare Economics to provide a sound and effective 'scientific' basis for normative-ethical statements which are firmly rooted in economic theory has not and most likely cannot be fulfilled. No stratagem, however clever, can build a solid bridge between positive and normative statements.

Welfare economics, including the 'New Welfare Economics', can only survive on the open or tacit ethical presumption that a greater amount of material goods means higher individual utility and that an increase in individual utility is a desirable aim. Since this utilitarian heritage can be found in and is accepted by a wide spectrum of psychological and ethical beliefs, it provides a useful and fruitful basis for normative discussions and for the attainment of consensus decisions. Insofar as welfare economics openly admits that it works on this ethical basis, its statements are acceptable and can serve as a valuable aid for socio-political discussions.

The trouble starts when some of the representatives of the New Welfare Economics try to underplay the normative elements in an attempt to increase the scientific image of the theory and to give the impression that the statements of welfare economics have the full weight of 'objective expert' knowledge. This can lead to two different problems. On the one hand it creates a tendency to regard the embodied ethical elements as central and self-evident and to neglect the existence of other, partly competing, ethical and ideological desiderata (including non-material, extra-market values). A proper consideration of these could lead to a modification of welfare economic prescriptions and could rob them of their commanding character. The second problem is a consequence of the steady – but finally futile – endeavour to cut out all social facts, no matter how relevant they may be, which cannot be submitted to rigid scientific methods of analysis and testing. Understandable as such a tendency is when adherence to the scientific-theoretical image is predominant, it nevertheless undermines the *raison d'être* of a welfare economics. The fact that some important elements cannot be treated as 'theoretically' as one would like does not preclude discussion of them in a reasonable way so that they are not neglected when it comes to reaching practical decisions.

A telling example of this refusal to consider 'soft' facts is the strict abstinence of New Welfare Economics with regard to all aspects concerning interpersonal comparisons of utility. Quite apart from the fact that such a strict adherence to methodological purity is not the general rule in the practice of social science,[10] it becomes particularly problematic in a branch which is bent on obtaining normative judgements for the real world. The fear of transgressing scientific boundaries – so typical of New Welfare Economics – has led to a remoteness from reality which seriously reduces its intended theoretical influence on practical affairs. It is not surprising that welfare economics has occasionally been criticized as being a 'nirvana' approach which does not facilitate access to the treatment of real problems.

These weak points of the New Welfare Economics suggest that it might be worth while to look for approaches capable of reaching fuller and more specific aids for concrete recommendations while still maintaining a high degree of economic competence. These approaches could still be based on openly declared utilitarian (or other) ethical principles, but could be enriched through additional non-economic considerations. Two possibilities will be discussed in the two following chapters. In Chapter 7 the question is raised whether it might not be possible to arrive at meaningful interpersonal comparisons of utility. If this were possible one could return to more significant statements such as were typical in the Old Welfare Economics without perpetuating its mistakes of treating certain value statements as self-evident truths or of presenting them in semi-factual forms. Chapter 8 deals with aspects of cost-benefit analysis which can be seen as a different attempt to combine economic and ethical-political elements in a suitable form for decision-making by foregoing the strict and demanding methodological requirements of welfare economics.

Appendix: a note on the impossibility theorem

This note is meant to present the main ideas of Arrow's impossibility theorem which has been mentioned above. Arrow put the question of whether it is possible to derive a 'democratic' aggregate social welfare function (or social preference function) from individual preferences which would consistently conform to the usual requirements of utility functions. Cardinal measurement is not required; all that is necessary is to be able to distinguish clearly three possibilities whenever a choice between alternatives has to be made. If x and y are two alternatives, the three possibilities are $x > y$ or $y > x$ or $x = y$ where $>$ stands for 'preferred over' and $=$ stands for 'indifferent to'.

Arrow lists four conditions which in his opinion have to be met if the social preference function is to be regarded as a 'true' (consistent) transformation of individual preferences. These four conditions are:

1. **Collective rationality:** The social preference function must display all the 'rational' characteristics of individual preference functions; that is, it must be unequivocal, complete and transitive. This means that all existing alternatives can be ordered and transitivity

is assured. In other words, when $x > y$ and $y > z$ we must also get $x > z$.

2. **Pareto principle:** This very plausible principle merely postulates that when $x > y$ is true for all individuals, $x > y$ should also be true for the social preference function.
3. **Independence of irrelevant alternatives:** The ordering between *given* alternatives x and y should only depend on individual preferences between these two alternatives and not be influenced by a changed context. Let us say we are concerned with the preference ordering between beer (B), white wine (W) and red wine (R). At a reception beer and red wine may be offered as drinks and one chooses red wine because one regards it as 'healthier' than beer: $R > B$. At another occasion one is invited to a meal and one is asked to choose between white and red wine. With an eye on the meal one chooses white wine: $W > R$. Following the transitivity rule we should conclude that $W > B$. However this does not follow. $B > W$ is just as possible when these two are presented in isolation (or in other special contexts).
4. **Non-dictatorship:** There is no individual whose preferences are automatically society's preferences independent of the preferences of all other individuals.

It can be shown that these four postulates can only be met under extremely unlikely conditions (for instance, when all individuals have identical utility functions). This means that normally a social preference function cannot be constructed. It can, of course, be objected that Arrow's four conditions present too high a standard in postulating that there should be a *direct* connection and correspondence between *all* individual preferences and the social preference function. However, this high standard finds justification insofar as it is in line with the methodological premises of the New Welfare Economics which 'prohibit' the recommendation of changes if they have negative effects on even a single person.

But even when we are prepared to take a more modest course than Arrow and to accept as aggregated social preference a function which can be obtained in a democratic process of decision-making, we have not got rid of all the difficulties of obtaining unique and consistent results. This is so because the preference ordering emerging from a democratic voting procedure is not independent of the circumstances under which the voting takes place. This can be shown by the following two examples.

In the first example, the so-called 'voting paradox', we assume that there are three alternatives under discussion, x, y and z, and that the population is divided into three groups of equal size, A, B and C, whose preferences are as follows:

$$A\colon\ x > y > z$$
$$B\colon\ y > z > x$$
$$C\colon\ z > x > y$$

Let us assume that only one of two alternatives is to be selected. If the choice is between x and y, a majority will vote for x ($A + C$): we obtain $x > y$; if y and z come up $A + B$ will give priority to y: $y > z$; finally if x and z are compared the votes of $B + C$ lead to $z > x$. However this result is a contradiction of the 'rational' transitivity rule which implies that if $x > y > z$ is valid, we should obtain $x > z$.

The second example shows that 'wrong' results can occur through manipulation. We start again with persons in three equally-sized groups, A, B and C, but take a situation where one out of four alternatives, w, x, y and z, is to be chosen. The voters can order their preferences by giving four points to their most preferred alternative, three points to the second best and so on. The alternative which obtains the highest number of points is to be accepted. The following table contains the preference patterns of the three groups:

	Points			
	4	3	2	1
A	*w*	*x*	*y*	*z*
B	*x*	*w*	*y*	*z*
C	*z*	*w*	*x*	*y*

In a normal voting process in line with these 'true' preferences, *w* would obtain ten points and would be the winning alternative. But suppose now that the *B*-group knows the preferences of the two other groups ('transparence'). It can then manipulate the result in its own favour by giving false information about its own preferences. By exchanging *w* with *z* in its voting paper, it can make *x* (with nine points) the winning alternative in place of *w*.

Of course the impossibility theorem and voting paradoxes do not imply that it is impossible to achieve workable political and ethical compromises when alternative policies are discussed. They only show that these 'solutions' cannot be obtained through 'theoretically' derived social welfare functions or other 'strictly theoretic' approaches to an optimum optimorum.

Notes

1. The two following quotations can be seen as examples of such 'robust' statements: 'As human nature is constituted, man rapidly degenerates unless he has some hard work to do' (A. Marshall); 'All human enjoyments tend to pall rapidly when repeated' (F. Taussig). These two examples are taken from a paper by R. Cooter and P. Rappoport (1984), 'Were the ordinalists wrong about welfare economics?', *Journal of Economic Literature*, **22** (2), June. After mentioning the above quotations the two authors continue: 'Such passages are relics of the prose style of 19th century British classics, which modern economists can find embarrassing, like a photograph from adolescence' (p. 520).

2. L. Robbins (1932), *An Essay on the Nature and Significance of Economic Science*, London: Macmillan.
3. Alternatively the 'core' can be defined as that set of Pareto-optimal constellations in which no person or coalition of persons can improve their position through independence (refusal to participate in the exchange process).
4. See J. de V. Graaf (1957), *Theoretical Welfare Economics*, London: Cambridge University Press.
5. A. Bergson (1938), 'A reformulation of certain aspects of welfare economics', *Quarterly Journal of Economics*, **52** (1), February.
6. K. J. Arrow (1951/1963), *Social Choice and Individual Values*, New York: Wiley. A short description of the impossibility theorem is given in the Appendix to this chapter.
7. N. Kaldor (1939), 'Welfare propositions in economics and interpersonal comparisons of utility', *Economic Journal*, **49** (3), September; J. R. Hicks (1939), 'The foundations of welfare economics', *Economic Journal*, **49** (4), December.
8. T. Scitovsky (1941), 'A note on welfare propositions in economics', *Review of Economic Studies*, **9** (1), November.
9. The impossibility of deriving definite priorities between Q and R in Figure 6.6 corresponds to the difficulties which can arise in welfare comparisons on the basis of revealed expenditure changes when market prices and quantities have changed. Writing P for price and Q for quantity indices, using subscripts 1 and 2 for two different periods and assuming that the total budget is spent on consumption, then a comparison of the two periods can yield one of the following four alternative constellations:

   1. $\Sigma P_2Q_2 > \Sigma P_2Q_1$
      $\Sigma P_1Q_1 < \Sigma P_1Q_2$
   2. $\Sigma P_1Q_1 > \Sigma P_1Q_2$
      $\Sigma P_2Q_2 < \Sigma P_2Q_1$
   3. $\Sigma P_2Q_2 < \Sigma P_2Q_1$
      $\Sigma P_1Q_1 < \Sigma P_1Q_2$
   4. $\Sigma P_2Q_2 > \Sigma P_2Q_1$
      $\Sigma P_1Q_1 > \Sigma P_1Q_2$

   In case (1) the person or group concerned prefers to buy basket Q_2 in period 2 although it could also have afforded at ruling prices (P_2) to buy the basket of period 1 (Q_1). At the same time we see that they were not able at the prices ruling in the previous period (P_1) to buy Q_2. If preferences are taken as given, this indicates an increase in welfare in period 2: preference for Q_2 is revealed and this preference could only be satisfied in the second period. Case (2) presents the exact opposite: Q_1 which was preferred to Q_2 in period 1 (when both baskets were within reach) can no longer be afforded in period 2. The switch to Q_2 therefore represents a reduction in welfare. Case (3) corresponds to the Scitovsky case.

The prices in period 1 permit the purchase of Q_1 but not that of Q_2 and vice versa in period 2 when only Q_2 but not Q_1 can be afforded. No preference is revealed and no ordering between the two periods is possible. Case (4) where different baskets are bought in the two periods, although a purchase of the alternative basket is also possible in both situations, is an expression of either a change in preferences or of spontaneous, 'irrational' purchasing behaviour.

10. D. McCloskey (*The Rhetoric of Economics*, Brighton: Wheatsheaf, 1985) has shown that economic theory has always supplemented strict analysis by other methods including *ad hoc* assumptions, plausibility arguments, conviction, etc.

7. Interpersonal Comparisons of Utility

Chapter 6 has shown how deep an impact the attacks by Robbins and others on the 'unscientific nature' of interpersonal comparisons of utility had on the theoretical ambitions of the Old Welfare Economics. Though no exception was taken to the underlying utilitarian ethics and the orientation towards efficiency values, the scope for 'scientific' or 'theoretical' welfare economic statements was considerably reduced.

The answer to this new situation could take three forms:

1. because of the difficulties pointed out, one could renounce all attempts at making normative statements and recommendations from a theoretical point of view. This would mean abolishing welfare economics altogether;
2. one could try to develop a new basis for welfare economics which could find its way without making interpersonal comparisons of utility; or
3. one could try to develop methods which would allow a 'scientifically acceptable' treatment of questions concerning interpersonal comparisons of utility so that a continuation of welfare economic studies in the tradition of the Old Welfare Economics would be possible.

Formally and in principle, strategies (1) and (2) have made the race. Economic theorists and theoretical economic literature normally adhere to one of these two alternatives.

As far as strategy (1) is concerned, this is simply a continuation of the old demand for a completely 'value-free' theory, the significance and difficulties of which we have discussed in Chapter 3. Strategy (2) led to the New Welfare Economics which – as we saw in the preceding chapter – had to pay for this 'scientific purification' by a loss of relevance and scope. Both these strategies present a serious problem. Whenever the one or the other is chosen we find that *in practice* many, if not all, economists cannot completely avoid introducing normative and recommendatory elements from time to time even when dealing with situations in which some groups of people suffer losses, so that an implicit comparison of preferences, utilities and advantages between different persons actually takes place. As long as this occurs in political discussions and with an open declaration of one's value premises, this constitutes no problem. But a problem does arise when these statements are interwoven with theoretical considerations masquerading as 'expert knowledge'. This danger is often present in view of the frequent (and in principle desirable) close connection between theoretical analysis and policy questions.

For these reasons and also because of the understandable wish to combine expert knowledge with relevant advice, it seems worthwhile to pay more attention to strategy (3) in order to see whether it might not be possible to find ways and means of providing a fairly 'solid' basis for reasonable discussions regarding interpersonal comparisons of utility. This will now be done.

As a start it will be useful to provide a more detailed account of the main objections *against* interpersonal comparisons of utility (ICU hereafter). This will give us a suitable critical background for the ensuing discussion of possible positive 'solutions'.

The theoretical objections against ICUs can be divided into four partly overlapping groups. A standard objection is the assertion that it is impossible to find a method for providing objective proofs in disputes about ICUs. Though a statement like 'good X will provide more utility for A than for B' sounds like a factual statement, it is in reality a subjective opinion. ICUs have therefore to be excluded if the Wertfreiheit-postulate is accepted. A second group of objections which is not quite so strict, points out that ICUs are normally not based on firm facts but have to depend on certain conventions (such as the assumption of identical capacities for satisfaction among all individuals). With regard to this objection however, one should note that such 'as if' conventions are widely used in theoretical studies (for instance, the assumption of general rational behaviour). Another view does not assert that ICUs are impossible in principle but suggests that this complex and difficult area should be left to other social sciences (such as psychology or sociology) since economic theory is more concerned with individual behaviour in the market and its effects on production and prices. ICUs only become important when the discussion moves to the desirability of alternative income distributions and this – so the argument runs – belongs to the realms of politics or sociology. Finally we come to a fourth group of objections which can be regarded as theoretically the most significant one. Here the negative attitude rests exclusively on the undeniable fact that no *secure* basis exists for scientific ICU statements. Some proponents in this group, the 'hardliners', maintain that ICU tests are impossible by nature, while a 'softer' view only says that *reliable* proofs are not attainable. The first view follows either from a narrow positivistic methodology which admits as 'scientific' evidence only directly observable and measurable phenomena, or it refers to the difficulties of extending the scientific debate beyond subjective and semi-subjective opinions whose differences cannot be bridged by testable statements. The 'softer' section regards rational and meaningful interpersonal discussions of ICUs based on various observations (physiological, interviews, etc.) as possible, but denies that they can be applied scientifically; this is because the limitations and weaknesses of the various indicators which are available make it impossible to arrive at definitive and reliable results. According to this argument, 'utility', which can only be approached indirectly, remains too vague a phenomenon to be compared between persons.

Confronted with this background of critical voices, one has at once to admit that there cannot exist any easy road to ICUs and that any statements regarding them must necessarily be 'soft' statements. If very high methodological standards are demanded from theoretical work, then it might be advisable to cut out ICUs completely. But the question of how ambitious the demands should be in the 'soft' sciences (to which the social sciences unfortunately must belong) cannot be decided solely on methodological grounds; relevance and the requirements of the phenomena under investigation should also be taken into account. If some relationships are very relevant for a given problem, it will be more efficient – not only for practical reasons but theoretically as well – to try to tackle these relationships with incomplete methods ('the best we have' as Schumpeter said) rather than disregard them altogether.

To take an example from another sector of economic science, let us look at the use we make of gross domestic product (GDP) measurements. GDP is not a unique, clear-cut 'real' phenomenon but an economic meaningful aggregate which is calculated according to generally accepted conventions. *Normally* we are quite prepared to equate the ups and downs of this indicator with 'improvements' or 'deteriorations' in the economy although we know that structural shifts, the ecological problem, distributional effects, etc. often permit very different interpretations of a *given* change in the GDP. The need to have *some* indicator for aggregate economic changes justifies the use of a 'sub-optimal' index like the GDP, though it would be dangerous to forget its limitations and weaknesses. We can look in a similar way at ICUs. If one is prepared to regard questions of welfare economics and income distribution as relevant candidates for theoretical investigation, then a complete repudiation of ICUs becomes a questionable strategy. A search for acceptable, though *unavoidably* incomplete and unsatisfactory, indicators makes sense.

When one turns to the task of finding some access to ICUs, it seems that a first step should be to find a clear definition of U: one should be clear about the meaning of utility which is to be used. Considering the importance of utility in economic theory in general, this is a theme whose importance stretches far beyond welfare economics and which deserves serious discussion. But it need not concern us here. No matter how one wants to define 'utility' – as the intensity of preferences, as expected or effective satisfaction, as happiness or contentedness, or as a momentary or long-term state of conscience – the problems connected with *interpersonal comparisons* remain more or less unaffected by these differences in definition. Their main difficulty consists in the fact that the subject one wants to investigate – utility – cannot be observed directly. Some of the factors connected with utility are 'visible' (such as willingness to pay, body temperature, etc.), but others are hidden inside the individual and not directly accessible. All one can hope for is to obtain a sufficient number of 'reasonable' indicators which will permit a fruitful discussion; exact measurements or unequivocal final results cannot be expected.

The basic problem for ICU is, of course, the heterogeneity of men, the variance of their preferences and capacities for satisfaction. If one is mesmerized by these differences, all hopes for ICU must be abandoned. But the question is whether these differences are so deep and so serious that they exclude any possibility of arriving at some generalizations regarding utility and satisfaction. After all we find that people within similar cultural and economic environments are – notwithstanding extreme individual deviations – not that different when we look at their principal needs, preferences and satisfactions. 'Menschen, Menschen sind wir alle' says an old Viennese song which can give us reason to accept as an *assumption* that a certain degree of uniformity exists. In a similar way economic theory acts on the assumption that all people behave like the homo oeconomicus, although we know that this is not generally true.

It is therefore understandable and justifiable that attempts at ICUs normally start with an assumption of (approximately) identical basic preference and utility structures of all persons. Of course, other assumptions could be chosen as a preliminary standard, but some plausible arguments in favour of the uniformity assumption can be produced. One argument has already been mentioned; the actual experience that the preferences of people living in similar environments show obvious similarities. Once this similarity is acknowledged, the *assumption* of identical preferences seems – as Harsanyi has stressed – 'justified'. That this assumption is inadmissable would now have to be proved by 'the other side' which regards the difference as too weighty. The uniformity assumption also has the advantage of simplicity, as Tinbergen has emphasized. A well-known methodological principle postulates that simple approaches are to be preferred when more complex alternatives cannot produce better results. Another reason was adopted by Lerner who based his uniformity hypothesis on a theorem of Leibniz which refers to the equi-probability of non-identifiable factors.

But the uniformity assumption can only serve as a starting point or as a 'bench mark'; it cannot be taken as a substitute for further analyses of utilities and utility differences. For these various indicators have to be created, investigated and critically scrutinized. The role of the uniformity assumption is to give meaning to these analyses by suggesting that the chosen indicators have a comparable relevance for different persons. This corresponds to the logic which also lies behind comparisons of regional and national welfare standards with the aid of social indicators.

The difficulty of finding significant indicators for utility purposes lies in the complexity and partial non-observability of the decisive influences. It cannot be expected that simple methods and simple indicators can be devised which will do the job. The following rough grouping of various (non-exclusive) approaches should give an idea of the variety of methods which can be used in the attempt to give ICU discussions a working basis.

A basic and traditional approach for comparisons of needs, utility and satisfactions of different persons uses a method of 'Verstehen' (understanding). It relies on the capacity to make genuine comparisons on the basis of introspection, sympathy and empathy which enable us to obtain insights into other people's feelings which can be rationally communicated and discussed. Take for instance a statement like the following: 'I believe that my visit to the opera means more to me than your tennis match means to you'. Such a statement is possible even if I care little for tennis and operas fail to interest my friend. 'Empathy' enables us to form ideas about other people's states of mind and preferences; we are thus able to make ICUs which are certainly not strictly testable or provable, but which are not meaningless.

In discussions with other people who are also 'empathetic', they can lead to a certain consensus which can be relevant for welfare economic considerations. That a chunk of bread can bring more utility to a starving person than an additional visit to the cinema to a well-off person will be an acceptable view to most people. In cases where the differences between the situations are less extreme, ICUs necessarily become more difficult and unreliable, but they are not impossible.

More concrete than this method of 'Verstehen' are indicators relating to material factors which are normally relevant for the provision of satisfactions. Income and wealth are prominent members in this group, but other means of obtaining goods and services can also be considered. Here we deal with observable and measurable items which can build a bridge for an approximation to invisible phenomena like needs, utilities and satisfactions. Accepting an approximate uniformity axiom and coupling it with the law of diminishing utility, we are led immediately to the utilitarian-welfare economic conclusion that a certain levelling of incomes (for instance through a progressive income tax) will imply a gain in general utility. A very simple model to this effect has the following form (following Tinbergen). Equation 7.1 presents a simple utility function with U for utility and Y for income, k is a constant factor which – using the uniformity axiom – is identical for all individuals.

$$U = k \ln Y \tag{7.1}$$

Differentiating (7.1) we obtain

$$\frac{dU}{dY} = k \frac{1}{Y} \quad \text{or} \quad dU = k \frac{dY}{Y} \tag{7.2}$$

which means that under the assumptions we have made, *equal* changes in utility among different persons will flow from an equal *proportional* change in their income. Redistribution from the rich to the poor will therefore yield a net gain in utility because the (given) transfer sum represents a smaller proportion of income in the rich man's budget than in the poor man's.

Considerations of this sort do not depend on the extreme assumption of absolutely identical utility functions. Even if preferences show a certain variation, it will still be true that a redistribution from the rich to the poor will yield a net gain in utility as long as we assume that the distribution of individual preference structures is similar both among the rich and among the poor. The redistribution will now hit different individuals differently, but *on average* the positive result is maintained. Such *collective* utility comparisons – concerning groups rather than individuals – are more robust than comparisons between individuals (because k in 7.1 need no longer be assumed as uniform but can be stochastically distributed); also usually such collective comparisons are all that are needed in economic policy decisions. It was this type of consideration which played an important role in the Old Welfare Economics.

However, basing utility differences mainly on indices of material availabilities by themselves is too narrow. Systematic differences in preferences and in the capacity of deriving satisfaction are also connected with other factors such as age, climate, health, etc. These influence the forms and intensity which income effects can have on utility levels. These factors also need consideration and, though this can be done to some extent, it is obvious that these additions complicate the picture and increase the range of possible (and uncertain) results.

Another attempt to base ICUs on objective indicators turns for help to the realms of psychology and biology. Some useful ideas from these areas can be obtained from studies about hierarchies of needs which try to structure them according to intensity rather than regard all needs as possible competitors without further differentiation between them, as is the practice in economic theory. That quenching one's thirst is a more intensive urge (and therefore more utility creating) than appeasing one's hunger and that this in turn takes priority over looking for shelter may be a fairly objective truth, but it does not take us very far. Once we leave this sphere of basic needs, a lexicographic (hierarchical) ordering of preferences becomes far less concrete and reliable. One example is Maslow's hierarchy of needs which starts with physiological needs followed by (in this order) safety needs, belonging and love needs, esteem needs and self-actualizing needs. In spite of their weak basis, biological and psychological approaches can play a certain role in rough comparisons or as supplementary material.

Still another group of indicators can be obtained by methods which are more familiar to economists, namely by attempts to derive conclusions from revealed preferences. Actual market behaviour can be used to obtain pointers regarding the relative importance of various needs and satisfactions. Demand structures and willingness to pay are obvious aids in this process, though it is not always easy to eliminate the influence of differences in purchasing power when one wants to concentrate on utilities. In addition to monetary demand, other related factors can also be used such as formation of queues, urgency of demand behaviour, criticisms, protest, etc.[1] The attempt to extract information on preferences and valuations from market phenomena also plays a part in cost-benefit analysis which will be taken up in the following chapter.

Finally some information can be obtained from 'hard' sciences, at least as subsidiary material, though not to the extent one would wish for in the interest of a more 'objective' foundation for ICUs. This group mainly comprises observable physiological and psychological phenomena which permit certain inferences regarding positive and negative utilities ('pleasure and pain'). Examples could include pulse rate and brain measurements, but also tears, blushing, facial expressions and body language. In view of different individual modes of reaction, which are also influenced by socio-cultural factors, the interpretation of such indicators is not easy. They, too, can at best only provide some approximative hints.

All these considerations point to an undeniable fact: ICUs are a complicated and difficult affair. The 'vagueness' and complexity of the problem make it impossible to obtain clear-cut, unequivocal indices and results. Yet at the same time ICUs are such an important element if welfare economics is to arrive at relevant valuations and conclusions that it seems justified to attempt answers in this field even when the data and methods used are far from perfect. There exists no royal road to 'correct' answers, but it is not impossible to collect material which provides a basis for 'rational' debate. The way will be replete with a 'multi-measurement-mix', the combination of several indices, observations and interviews whose critical interpretation can lead to cautious compromises in utility comparisons. If this sounds too 'unscientific' one should remember that quite a number of widely applied and accepted 'economic-theoretical' statements and recommendations also rest on hypotheses which have rather shaky foundations but whose interpretation and usefulness have been 'hardened' in a continuing process of discussion and modification. Contents and welfare implications of such entities as GDP, economic growth, efficiency and ecology can be named as examples.[2]

I conclude this chapter with a more concrete illustration of possible strategies. To do this I give a short account of a comparative study on work satisfaction[3] which comes up against the same problems of 'non-visibility' and absence of objective scales of measurement as are met in utility comparisons in general. At the beginning of that study one had first to agree on the factors which have an important influence on work satisfaction in order to subject these to detailed scrutiny. This choice of decisive factors was of course not quite arbitrary; it could draw on existing experiences and previous studies. As a result, the following six factors were chosen:

1. Management
2. Fellow workers
3. Job content
4. Wages
5. Career opportunities
6. Working time

Each of these basic factors was then fitted into the analysis by various descriptive methods which were subjected to numerical scales wherever possible. Examples of such indicators were for instance: for (1) contact opportunities, codetermination, praise and reproof; for (2) degree of acceptance by fellow workers; for (3) monotony, stress, learning opportunities, for (4) absolute and relative wages, for (6) total working time, intervals and flexibility.

The importance of these factors and their changes for work satisfaction and its intensity were then compressed into combined indicators which were obtained through a whole battery of 'objective' and 'subjective' tests. Objective tests included comparative analyses of fluctuations, accidents, productivity and absenteeism; subjective tests consisted mainly of sophisticated questionnaires and interviews which provided hypotheses for ordinal preference scales. In this way a broad basis of diverse material was obtained which could then be used for comparative statements regarding work satisfaction. These were followed up by comparisons with other indices and observations which could be regarded as relevant information. In this way results were achieved which could be 'reasonably' discussed, criticized and modified by wider circles of scientists and other persons who had not been involved in the original investigation. Even so, such results remained only approximative hints without any firm proofs. But they could be at least partly 'convincing' and as such assist public discussion and decision-making (where anyway usually only rough comparisons are considered) in a way a welfare economics which rejects every attempt in this direction as 'unscientific' cannot attain.

Notes

1. Alternative reactions to economic processes are analysed in A. O. Hirschman (1970), *Exit, Voice and Loyalty*, Cambridge, Mass.: Harvard University Press.
2. See footnote 10 of Chapter 6.

3. See J. L. Simon (1974), 'Interpersonal welfare comparisons can be made – and used for redistribution decisions' *Kyklos*, **27** (1), March. The comparison discussed in the text was carried out in studies on work motivation by Vroom.

8. Cost-Benefit Analysis

The last two chapters have shown that there is no simple way to overcome the basic dilemma of the New Welfare Economics following from the desire to combine rigid methodological (positivistic) rules with utilitarian-based, ethically relevant statements for practical affairs. The principle of *potential* compensation reduces a large proportion of possible answers to practical irrelevancy; the construction of social preference functions comes up against the impossibility theorem, and attempts at interpersonal comparisons of utility are – even if not excluded outright – extremely difficult and can at best lead to ambiguous results.

In view of this situation it would seem worthwhile to look for other, theoretically less demanding, methods which would allow economists to use their expertise – perhaps in cooperation with other scientists – to find more pragmatic ways of producing the sorts of statements and recommendations which are the aim of welfare economics. One such possibility can be seen in the techniques of Cost-Benefit Analysis (CBA). Cost-Benefit Analysis is a tool for decision-making processes which was created mainly by economists and which is based more on practical-pragmatic considerations than on a fully defined theoretical structure. Its main purpose is to provide supplementary material for plans which cannot be decided solely on the basis of market data; that is, by comparing monetary costs and revenues of a project in a balance sheet. If market results cannot be accepted as the only criterion of 'efficiency' and 'rationality' because non-market factors also play an important role, then CBA is a method which tries to find quantitative estimates for these missing items so that a decision can be taken on the basis of an extended, more complete balance sheet.

The values one has to find for the items which have no market price (or comparable valuation) can be obtained by various methods. These methods need not necessarily be the responsibility of economists. Yet the fact that economists are used to thinking in terms of credits and debts, valuations and 'efficiency', has meant that they more than other scientists have promoted and used CBA methods. The question is therefore justified whether their specific knowledge of this area – of the problems, possibilities and pitfalls – does not qualify them *as experts* to contribute decisive statements on policy matters, including those which contain welfare and ethical elements.

The idea of CBA was born because of the need for decisional aids in the sphere of public investment, particularly 'big' investments of the infrastructure type (transport, communication, health, education, etc.). While it is fairly simple to calculate the costs of such projects, it is difficult to form concrete ideas about the value of their output. This is so partly because the output is not sold on the market and partly because of the important external effects of such investments which also need consideration. CBA is the attempt to find 'rational' methods for a (market-type) evaluation of these items in monetary terms so that it becomes possible to judge and compare the 'profitability' of various potential projects. Insofar as one is prepared to accept genuine and/or simulated market prices as suitable indicators of societal values (a view implied in several sectors of traditional economic theory), CBA facilitates pragmatic access to calculations which can be helpful for judging levels of 'social welfare'.

Public investment decisions have remained the main field for CBA. But in addition to this other applications have come into use. CBA plays a certain role in management science when considerations extend beyond the 'classical' balance sheet and try to include such imponderables as good will, standing of the firm, and other non-market aspects. Important from our point of view is that CBA can also be used for fairly wide definitions of social targets by including ethical items, considerations of long-term developments, etc. CBA can be regarded as a means to give these considerations concrete weights when it comes to deciding on and between various projects. This fact makes it desirable for us to take a closer look at the possibilities and limits of CBA.

It has already been stressed that CBA does not rest on a clear-cut theoretical structure but relies on more pragmatic approaches. Accordingly there are no hard and fast rules as to how CBA should proceed. The basic idea is clear. A way is to be found which permits – through evaluation of all relevant items – the establishment of a comprehensive income-expenditure ('profit-loss') account whose balance can serve as a basis for decisions. A positive balance points to the worthwhile-ness of a project: a bigger balance for project *A* than for project *B* suggests that *A* should be preferred. But while this basic idea is simple enough, difficulties and uncertainties arise in its execution. Several questions remain open: which items are to be included in the calculations; how are the different items to be evaluated (such as time saved through wider roads); which discount rate should be used for future benefits (such as oil reserves in 50 years) etc. It will be obvious that there can be no generally valid answers to these questions. They will depend on the nature of the problem under discussion and on actual circumstances, but will also be influenced by aims and ideas regarding efficiency, ethical implications, etc. so that a perfectly 'objective' procedure can hardly be expected. To some extent the last-mentioned problem can be mitigated by declaring one's 'biases' so that they can be taken into account when the results are discussed.

If (and as far as) CBA wants to keep in line with the main ideas of the New Welfare Economics, it will base its considerations – at least in principle – on indicators of individual utility (backed by purchasing power) and on the principle of *potential* compensation. If for instance a project P which cannot be marketed (such as a public good) is under debate, one would 'ideally' want two alternative sets of information. For people who favour the project, one would like to know the maximal sum S_1 which they would be prepared to pay in order to get P carried out; in the case of people who object to P, one would need to know the minimum sum S_2 which would induce them to accept P. Summing all individual S_1 to $\bar{S}_1$ and all individual S_2 to $\bar{S}_2$ and calculating the balance $D = \bar{S}_1 - \bar{S}_2$, one comes to a positive evaluation of the project when the balance is positive ($D > 0$) because it is then possible in principle (though not necessarily in practice) to compensate all those who object while still leaving some gain of utility for supporters. In case of a choice between different projects, say P_i and P_j, P_i should be preferred to P_j when $D_i > D_j$ and vice versa.

CBA in this form displays a close relationship with the New Welfare Economics, at least in principle. But an important advantage of the CBA approach is that it encompasses wider perspectives both with regard to the items to be considered and to methods of evaluation. The ties to market processes are not as binding and a broader view of utility can be adopted, allowing more room for social and ethical considerations if this is desired. The treatment of problems where ethics and economics overlap seems to become more accessible. But a host of new problems arise. How is utility to be estimated in the more 'delicate' and 'soft' sectors? How far is willingness to pay (with its dependence on income and wealth and a diminishing marginal utility of money) a suitable indicator for a broad calculation of utility and social welfare? Should some items be given different weights for different groups (rich and poor), and how far should ethical considerations affect the weights (should envy be counted as a 'cost' in terms of utilities)? What about discounting the utilities of future generations? How far are compensations an effective possibility?[1]

All these questions are touched upon to some degree in almost every CBA, but they become particularly weighty when one deals with projects and problems concerning important social and ethical aspects like health, education and social status. In view of the weak theoretical basis of CBA, different strategies can be chosen when faced with these difficulties. At one extreme one can decide to dispense with CBA altogether except in the easier cases of management problems or technical public projects of limited scope. At the other extreme stands the 'courageous' attempts to find some valuation in one way or another for all the items which are regarded as relevant including ethical and welfare items, so as to be able to arrive at a quantitative final result. Intermediate solutions restrict CBA to those decisive items which can be assessed by fairly reliable and accepted methods and leave the 'softer' factors, like ethical or ecological aspects, to subsequent discussions during which the CBA results can be modified.

None of these strategies is fully satisfactory because not one of them is able to master all the problems inherent in the CBA approach. An 'ideal solution' yielding unique and clear-cut monetary results which could serve as a reliable basis for decision-making founders on the arbitrariness of estimation methods and on the considerable variability of results which can be caused by even slight variations in the assumptions. In the Appendix to this chapter an illustration of this variability is given for the case of estimation procedures (inspired by economic-theoretical methods) concerning the value of human life in projects where human lives are endangered or can be saved. Even when the chosen method of estimation is presented in full detail (a practice which is not always observed) so that it can be critically judged and modified by other persons, the problem remains that the presentation of a certain monetary sum creates an impression of precision which cannot really be achieved. This problem is particularly pressing in the less tangible spheres of politics and ethics where value biases have already entered into the design and choice of estimation methods. This makes it difficult to arrive at truly 'objective' measurements.

If one tries to escape these problems by adopting the interim solution of leaving out of the CBA all the more critical items (such as valuations of human lives), one has a situation which can satisfy neither the optimists nor the sceptics. If one takes a very strict separation and includes only the 'hard' items in the CBA, leaving everything else to subsequent discussions, then one does not really advance very much beyond ordinary income-expenditure accounts. The aid one expects from CBA will then not materialize. If one tries to tackle some of the 'softer' items however the methodological uncertainties quickly become visible even if one is prepared to adhere as closely as possible to time-honoured economic approaches. Take for instance the case of increased risks of work accidents connected with a certain project. How should they be valuated? Should one measure them by the additional wages which workers may demand as compensation for the additional risks? Should one calculate the probable loss in production arising from accidents? Or should one use still other methods? Obviously there exists a different basic perspective behind each approach. Thus an interim solution which is not too restrictive cannot completely escape some of the ambiguities which are typical of 'ideal' approaches. At the same time it has the disadvantage of not being able to come up with a definite final result (whatever its quality may be).

Yet an absolute refusal to use CBA cannot be the optimal answer to all these difficulties. If we require certain ethical, ecological and other factors not reflected in market data to be considered in project decisions, then some evaluation of these items *must* take place, be it only by verbal and discursive methods. There is no way to avoid the problem of evaluation. Taking this into account one can see CBA as the attempt to 'translate' certain vague ideas into a somewhat more concrete, quantitative form in order to make them more tractable in complicated, multi-dimensional decision processes. If this can be done in a convincing way, CBA can be a useful aid in welfare economics and ethically relevant decisions. But it must never be forgotten that CBA, with its strong bias towards market valuations as a standard of efficiency, cannot claim to be representative of wider and more comprehensive definitions of individual and social welfare, let alone 'happiness'. Just like welfare economics, CBA cannot provide a 'theoretically based' bridge between expert and normative statements. If this fact is overlooked CBA can be turned into a one-sided semi-precise, semi-scientific 'expertocratic' instrument instead of providing beneficial information and help as part of a wider and open discussion.[2]

Appendix: Valuation of human lives

In the following paragraphs the extreme case of finding estimates for the value of human lives is presented as an illustration of the difficulties which are generally met when it comes to ascertaining monetary values for important non-market factors.

A preliminary question which arises when we deal with human lives or other important human or ecological damages is whether it makes sense even to attempt to put a monetary value on such phenomena. One ethical objection which is occasionally put forward holds that the 'holiness' of human life forbids one to express it in money terms. Understandable as such an objection is, it is nevertheless not valid. In many projects implicit ideas abut the 'value' of lives unavoidably enter into the decision process. Two cases can serve as an example: in deciding whether to purchase expensive medical equipment or to rebuild roads for greater traffic safety, the question of how many lives per year will probably be saved cannot be neglected. Costs are a barrier which inhibit the undertaking of many life-saving projects which would be possible in principle. Some evaluation of the importance of saving a life is therefore unavoidable even though it may only be implicit and vague because quantifications are resisted.

If a quantification is (or were) possible, it would offer the advantage that the implicit valuations could be spelled out and confronted more exactly with the expected costs. Economists with experience of CBA seem particularly suited to tackle such quantification problems, and most relevant attempts have come from this source. Yet the problems which one faces are considerable. Life is not a marketable good and there are no obvious alternative market signals which could serve as indicators for an evaluation. A purely positive economic theory can provide hardly any indication for a statement on this matter. But in the framework of CBA one can try to find a 'reasonable' method for constructing valuations which can then be a supporting element in the decision process. However all these methods are necessarily somehow 'artificial'. They must try – starting from their economic-theoretical experience – to obtain certain auxiliary indicators which can be used or combined for a 'telling' statement. Not surprisingly one finds that considerable discrepancies exist between results obtained by different methods. This in itself is not a decisive argument against such methodological experiments and calculations. But it is a warning that such calculations rest on debatable foundations and contain normative elements which have gone into (and are hidden in) the specific method applied.

What do these methods look like? There are quite a number of possible approaches, but by and large one can distinguish two types of groups: objective and subjective methods. The objective methods try to value a life on the basis of the objectively measurable opportunity costs which a lost life entails. This can be done either by calculating what has been lost or what expectations have had to be given up. Form and content of the calculations do not follow a definite pattern and are far from simple as far as data and assumptions are concerned. Thus for evaluating the loss of a human life the calculations may be based on expected and discounted non-fulfilled consumption (lost utility) or on lost future (discounted) production, or they may use lost human capital (investment of education, occupational experience, etc.) as a suitable indicator. Depending on the method chosen, results can be rather different. Moreover some delicate questions arise, as for instance whether it is defensible that the life of a wealthy consumer or of a highly qualified worker should be more highly valued than that of a less well-equipped person.

But a more fundamental objection from the point of view of economic methodology concerns the fact that these 'objective' methods are not in line with the traditional principles of welfare economics and CBA, which aim at a valuation of 'utility' on the basis of individual evaluations as they are revealed (within the constraints of purchasing power) in market transactions and prices or at least in simulated prices. As far as human lives are concerned, the decisive question is then not what the 'objective' individual or social *costs* of a lost life are, but what *value* an individual attaches to life; that is, how much he or she is prepared maximally to pay in order to reduce the risk of death. This perspective leads us to the second approach – subjective methodology.

A first step in this direction can consist in simply asking people what worth they attach to life. The question must be formulated carefully however. If it reads 'How much are you prepared to pay to keep your life instead of losing it [now]' people would probably go to the absolute limits of their possibilities. But in the projects which are subjected to CBA, we are not faced with such *certain individual* 'death sentences' but rather with *risks* of losing somebody's life when a certain project is not undertaken. The proper question should therefore be on the following lines: 'What sum would be necessary to induce you to drink out of this glass if there is a risk of $\frac{1}{1000}$ that it contains a lethal poison? If the answer is for instance £5 000, we can conclude on the basis of a calculation which will be explained below that this person's 'statistical' valuation of life amounts to £5 000 000. The weak point in this and other forms of questioning lies in the extreme arbitrariness and unreliability of the answers one obtains. Many people fail to appreciate the meaning of a certain risk. However, the main difficulty is that reactions to a riskless experimental situation which has no consequences may be totally different to what would happen if these people were faced with comparable real-world situations.

In order to circumvent this unreliability of interviews and questionnaires, an attempt has been made to develop methods which could use information from actual behavioural patterns in situations where risks to life *are* involved. In line with the economic tradition of looking to markets and prices as indicators or 'revealed' preferences, such information about risk valuation can come, for example, from insurance payments, from wage differentials between occupations involving different degrees of risk, from price differences between cars offering different degrees of security, etc.

There are different variants of this approach but their common basis can be summarized in the following question: 'How much is a representative individual prepared to pay to reduce a certain existing risk to life by Δr?'; alternatively, 'What additional payment can be demanded to make one willing to accept an additional risk of Δr?' Such payments or demands are in principle observable. The data so obtained can be used for the calculation of 'value of life' by a method based on the following considerations.

If we write V for the measure we are looking for, namely

the 'value of a human life', the formula used by this method (to be explained later) is

$$V = \frac{v}{r} \text{ or, } V = \frac{\Delta v}{\Delta r}$$

where r stands for the risk (per year) of losing one's life (Δr for a *change* in that risk), and v (Δv) for the sum (additional sum) an individual is prepared to pay in order to avoid that risk (or change in risk) or the sum which he/she demands in order to shoulder that risk or its increase. In the following examples we shall use the second formulation because it is more relevant to actual situations where we normally observe payments concerning additional risks.

Before explaining the 'meaning' which lies behind the above formula, it may be useful to show its 'working' by a numerical example. Let us assume that the 'normal' existing risk of dying during a certain period (say a year) for a given person is 8 per cent ($\frac{8}{100}$). There exists a possibility of reducing this risk by some means from 8 per cent to 7 per cent ($\frac{7}{100}$), involving a *change* in risk (Δr) of $\frac{1}{100}$. If, in addition to existing risk-reducing expenditures, the given person is prepared to pay an amount of £5 000 (i.e. Δv = 5 000) for this measure, then we obtain from our formula

$$V = \frac{\Delta v}{\Delta r} = \frac{5\,000}{\frac{1}{100}} = 500\,000$$

a value of life of £500 000.

What is the reasoning behind this calculation of V – the 'statistical value of life' as it is normally called? To explain it we shift from the case of an individual to a group of persons which is in any event plausible because in typical CBA cases and public projects, one is concerned with population groups. We assume that there is a group of n persons for whom a certain measure would imply a reduction in the risk of death by Δr per year for each person. This means that for the group as a whole each year, $\Delta r.n$ lives would be saved. Let us now further assume that people are prepared to pay on average Δv for the introduction of the risk-reducing measure. Then a total amount of $\Delta v.n$ can be obtained and we can calculate an average ('statistical') value *per life saved* by dividing total payments by total lives saved:

$$V = \frac{\Delta v.n}{\Delta r.n} = \frac{\Delta v}{\Delta r}.$$

Returning to our previous numerical example and expanding it to a group of 1000 persons ($n = 1000$) then we obtain – with $\Delta r = \frac{1}{100}$ – a saving of ten lives a year for which the group as a whole is prepared to pay £5 000 000 (5 000.n). This comes to £500 000 per life saved. This shows why this calculation is called the 'statistical' value of life.

It is not difficult to see that such a method can deliver results which differ radically from those obtained by the alternative methods mentioned earlier. But even when one decides to accept the 'statistical' approach as the proper method, one has not resolved all problems. Considerable uncertainties and differences in results remain. This is partly due to wide differences in individual attitudes to various kinds of risks and risk changes and also to the fact that risk situations are anything but transparent and easily understood. 'Normal' choice behaviour in this field corresponds even less to the 'rational' model of the coolly calculating homo oeconomicus than in other fields. The following cases are important typical examples of the problems to be faced.

If the real 'price' of life is to have a continually reliable value of, let us say, $\bar{V}$ (at least for a certain person or group of persons) and if the above method is correct, then we should expect that the sum people are prepared to pay for a reduction of risk should vary *proportionally* with the size of the reduction. Only if this is true will we obtain a reliable, unchanging valuation of life according to the formula $V = \frac{\Delta v}{\Delta r}$. But this proportionality is absent for two reasons. The first follows from the economic-psychological 'law' of diminishing marginal utility. Figure 8.1 refers to this case. 8.1(a) shows the conditions for a constant value $\bar{V}$. The abscissa of the diagram contains a scale for the risks to life (r), starting with a value of 1 (= 100 per cent certainty of death) and falling continually to zero (no risk whatsoever). On the ordinate the sum v is measured which people are prepared to pay to avoid risks. The curve $\bar{A}0$ shows a willingness to pay in proportion to the risks avoided; its slope $\frac{\Delta v}{\Delta r}$ is constant and so is $\bar{V}$.

Because of the law of diminishing marginal utility, people will be prepared to pay very high prices to obtain a certain reduction of very high risks, but will then be continually less willing to pay when the risks are lower; that is, when they already possess high quantities of the good 'risk reduction'. This case is illustrated in Figure 8.1(b). It shows that at very high risk levels surpassing the value of $\bar{r}$ (such as risks to life after being taken hostage), people will go to the limit of their possibilities in order to reduce that risk, but that very much less will be paid for additional reductions of smaller risks and perhaps nothing

Figure 8.1 *The diminishing marginal utility of risk reduction*

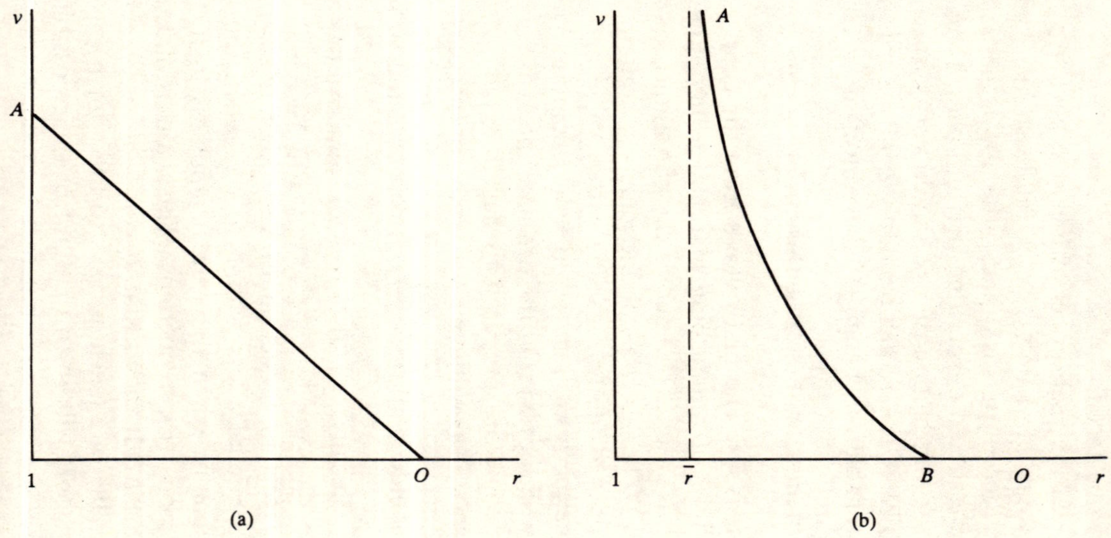

at all for reductions of very small risks (such as the purchase of additional headlights for the motor car to reduce the risk of accidents in foggy weather). Readiness to pay for risk reductions is therefore far from being proportional. It will be dependent on the level of existing risks; $\frac{\Delta v}{\Delta r}$ and with it V can take on very different values, as shown by curve AB in 8.1(b).

Another reason for the variability of V-values follows from the empirically established fact that people do not (or cannot) distinguish clearly between smaller and bigger reductions in risks. Experience shows that on the whole people are often prepared to pay *something* for the reduction of a certain perceived risk, even if the reduction is fairly small, but that they are not prepared to increase such payments *in proportion* for alternatives offering bigger reductions. This means that when different risk reduction alternatives are compared, one finds that Δv rises systematically less than Δr. As a consequence V varies depending on the specific alternative which is used for the calculation, being lower the higher the risk reduction potential of the given alternative. How extreme the consequences of this factor are can be shown in an experiment by P. Mulligan who tried to find out how much people would be prepared to pay for *alternative reductions* of risks from *given levels of risks* in atomic energy plants. The results and their effect on the statistical value of life are shown in the following table (in 1980 dollars, see opposite page).

Another not unimportant element refers to the fact that individual valuations or risk reductions do not depend only on the *amount* of risk reduction, but also on the *type* of risk. Thus, if we have a situation where 100 000 people living in 100 communities with 1 000 inhabitants each are threatened by a 1 per cent risk of additional deaths (= 1 000 people), this risk will be judged differently depending

Reduction in risk (Δr)	Readiness to pay (Δv)	Statistical value of life (V)
$\frac{1}{100\,000}$	35.76	3 576 000
$\frac{1}{10\,000}$	42.80	428 000
$\frac{1}{1\,000}$	62.00	62 000

on whether it is spread equally throughout the total population or whether it might focus on one single community.

We must conclude that the variety of methods for estimating values of life as well as the variance of results within each method create such latitude for calculations that the arbitrariness and the difficulties of interpretation are overwhelming. Thus, it is not surprising that a comparison of 11 American calculations of the value of a human life shows results ranging from \$66 000 to \$11.8 million (*Wall Street Journal*, 15 December 1988).

Notes

1. Probably no conceivable compensation could win acceptance for a project which would involve an almost certain risk of death for the person concerned. Yet the evaluation of elements which can have an important influence on marginal risks to life (e.g. purchase of expensive medical equipment as such or in competition with a project for improved education) are quite often part of cost-benefit calculations.
2. A compromise solution which is perhaps the best way to prevent a dubious quantification of non-market elements, is the use of cost-effectiveness analysis instead of CBA. Cost-effectiveness analysis also presents a balance sheet, but exact monetary values are only given on the cost side (where market data are available) while on the 'output' side the expected and relevant items are all listed but not quantified in monetary terms. This means of course that no monetary balance is obtained, but the difficulty of estimating the

sensitive items is made clear and handed over to the discussion process. A 'subjective' element remains, however, in the choice of items included in the list.

9. Income Distribution and Justice

In the first chapter it was mentioned that questions of justice represent a special aspect in the field of ethics. Justice is not so much concerned with individual action, with the 'good' individual, as with a 'good' ordering of human relations. Of course a 'just person' displays moral qualities, but he/she cannot by him/herself create a just order. This can only be achieved at the level of society as a whole. The economic system as a section of the total human network of relations can be judged – depending on one's ethical position – as 'just' or 'unjust'. This final chapter dealing with justice and income distribution is particularly relevant for the theme of the book because there are hardly any fields in economic theory or economic policy where a confrontation between ethical ideas and economic opinions becomes so visible and almost unavoidable. This was evident when the four typical and conflicting economic aims of the post-war era – economic growth, full employment, price stability and balance of payments equilibrium (the magic 'polygon') – were supplemented by the idea of a 'just income distribution' as a fifth item.[1]

Of course all these targets imply certain value judgements; this is a characteristic of every target. But while economic growth simply expresses the widely accepted utilitarian principle that more material wealth increases utility and is therefore desirable, and that full employment, price stability and balance of payments stability have a 'derived' desirability as instruments for achieving growth (with additional social elements in the employment target), it is only in connection with the distribution target that the ethical adjective 'just' is explicitly mentioned. This indicates a doubt whether market processes and economic-utilitarian perspectives are by themselves a sufficient basis for obtaining 'good' income distributions. Other criteria are obviously also required. This is so because distribution questions are *necessarily* connected with conflict situations. Questions of economic growth, fights against inflation, etc. can of course also lead to conflicts about forms and the extent of the steps to be taken; but it is only in the case of income distribution that conflicts are an *inherent* element of the problem. The distribution of the already produced output will normally lead to privileged and non-privileged groups, to 'winners' and 'losers'. Who is to be counted as belonging to the one group or to the other (or whether such groups exist at all) cannot be decided unless one has a certain standard for evaluation. One must be able to judge what is 'right': a standard for 'justice' is needed.

Remembering what we said in earlier chapters one could, of course, argue that while it is true that problems of justice are unavoidable in economic policy and political debates when such questions of income formation and taxation arise, the 'value-free' economic theorist could *qua* scientist side-step these debates and restrict himself to 'objective' descriptions and analyses of the actual distribution processes and their results. Without doubt this is to some extent the practice in theoretical literature. 'Pure' empirical and theoretical studies about functional and personal income distributions (the latter being particularly significant in relation to 'justice') have a long tradition and have produced valuable insights, even though not all questions can be regarded as 'solved'. But it is also a fact that in actual disputes and confrontations dealing with questions of income distribution, which cannot be free from conflicting ideas about justice, economists frequently enter the discussion and tend to make – *qua* experts! – statements and recommendations with obvious emotional undertones. When it comes to questions of achieving a 'just' distribution of incomes, bishops and economists are frequently seen to pull in different directions.

The main reason for *this* conflict (in contrast to the unavoidable conflict of the immediate parties in the distribution process) can be found in two elements: the 'double nature' of incomes on the one hand and a confrontation between differing ethical positions (not always made explicit) on the other. The 'double nature' of personal income consists in the fact that the (absolute and relative) income of a person (or family) determines the welfare (utility) and the social status of that person, but should at the same time act as a motivational stimulus for productivity and as an instrument for achieving a proper allocation of labour and capital over the various branches of the economy. If one is mainly concerned with the welfare and status of each and every person – a typical basis for humanistic ideas of justice – then one will tend to favour a 'philosophy' of income equality. Against this, income differentials may be regarded more favourably when one is concerned mainly with work incentives and structural adjustments to a dynamic economic process. This latter question – whether and to what extent income levels and income differentials have an effect on productivity and mobility – is a *factual* (though not easily answerable) question which economists are certainly competent to investigate in theoretical and quantitative terms. If they confined themselves to explaining and calculating the 'costs' in terms of lost growth and structural problems which various ethically and politically motivated reforms are likely to entail, no *decisional* conflict between economists and reformers would exist. The economic argument could (and should) be taken into account in making ethical-political decisions and that would be all.

This is not the usual picture however. Certain ideas and reform proposals concerning the distribution of income are frequently rejected 'on principle' by economists (and business interests) because they would be harmful to economic efficiency (economic growth and allocation). Proposals based on partial interests and/or on ethical ideas about justice are countered with 'theoretical' statements which demand special consideration. What looks like an expert judgement about 'correct' income distributions is in reality nothing but a confrontation between two value positions: a distribution target oriented on 'justice' facing a target oriented on 'efficiency'. Such a confrontation is a justifiable and important aspect of societal decision processes. But conflicting views should not be overruled unilaterally by the 'theoretical' viewpoint; the decision itself remains a political-ethical affair which can become more informed through expert advice and opinion but cannot obtain an 'objective' solution from this source alone.

Thus 'justice' and 'efficiency' have to be seen as potentially conflicting targets between which a certain trade-off will exist. With this trade-off in mind, a concrete and viable 'solution' can be worked out in an ethical-political-economic debate which will correspond more or less to this or that idea of justice and more or less to 'pure' ideas of economic efficiency. The rest of this chapter will deal with various aspects of this conflict and trade-off problem. But before we turn to these questions, it is important to note that in many cases such problems will not be relevant because in theory as well as in practice the two targets need not contradict each other; they can point in the same direction so that no confrontation exists. A few examples can show this.

If we start from an ethical idea that justice demands a more equal distribution of incomes (more on this target later) and assume that this leads to a corresponding redistribution of incomes (through taxes, transfers, etc.), the improvement of living standards among the poorer sections of the population can lead to an increase in their physical and learning efficiency, with positive effects on total output. Such a sequence can play a considerable role in developing countries. In developed industrial economies it will be less relevant, though improvements for lower income classes (including shorter working time, holidays and educational opportunities) may well lead to higher productivity by creating a greater capacity for meeting the growing demands and the stress of modern technology. As another example we might mention the role of widespread ideas of 'fairness' (more on this later). If very unequal income distributions are regarded as unfair, moves to a 'fairer' ('juster') distribution can have positive effects on work satisfaction and motivation. Business economists and psychologists are well aware that such parallel movements of 'justice' and 'efficiency' can play a role at the firm level. Among theoretical economists, however, in whose models price differences and price structures are the principal agents in the motivation and allocation process, one finds a certain tendency to regard all forms aimed at some levelling of incomes with distrust and as a probable source of efficiency losses.

All these unproblematic cases where justice and efficiency are in agreement will now be left behind as we turn to cases where ethical and economic ideas come into conflict. That ethical ideas of justice and the facts of economic life can create problems has been realized since antiquity. Important ideas were laid down by Aristoteles in his distinction between distributive and corrective justice, between justice in exchange and in distribution. In pre-industrial and pre-capitalistic days, when the incomes of most people belonging to the free population were either earned through self-employment in agriculture or rigidly fixed through traditional and guild ordinances, questions of justice became relevant mainly in relation to sales and purchases on the less regular and less regulated markets. Justice in exchange – the search for the 'just price' – stood at the centre of ethical disputes. Its importance in the scholastic literature of the Middle Ages is evident.

With the advance of the capitalist industrial society, with its huge division of labour and the growth of a dependent labour force, the weights were radically shifted from questions of exchange justice to those of a just distribution of incomes. Justice in exchange or questions about 'just' prices did not disappear altogether but quickly lost importance in view of the ubiquity of competitive markets where prices 'occurred' more or less automatically and anonymously. Objections against 'unjust' or 'too high' prices were raised mainly in connection with monopolistic practices of charging high prices and earning high profits. In this respect, however, no conflicts between ethical and economic value perspectives arise since monopoly pricing is also at odds with economists' postulates of allocative efficiency.

The idea of the 'just price' survived, however, in a new form; it became important as the search for a 'just wage' – a just price on the quickly expanding labour markets where the majority of the working population had to 'sell' their services. But in contrast to commodity prices, the price for labour (wages) is not just the basis for determining the terms of exchange in momentary but frequently recurring transactions; it usually takes the form of a long-term contract which has far-reaching consequences for the income, the living standard and the social status of an individual. The question of a 'just wage' therefore leads directly to questions about just incomes and 'just income distributions' which then are extended to a consideration of all incomes including income from land, capital (rents, profits) etc. This has meant that the problem of a just distribution of incomes has moved to the centre of ethical-economic dilemmas. This dilemma alone will be the subject of the following paragraphs.

In dealing with the differences and confrontations which exist in this field between ethics and economic theory, one is at once faced with the difficulty that both sides offer several views on the subject which are not only different but in some cases also contradictory. This plurality of views is particularly noticeable on the ethical side which is less hemmed in by the 'barriers' of reality than economics. In a book on income distribution[2] the Dutch economist Jan Pen has given a list of not less than 21 different views on 'just' and 'proper' income distributions held by various groups. They are partly unconnected, partly overlapping, and not seldom pointing in totally opposite directions. Leaving out some of the more outlandish ideas, the following choice from Pen's list indicates how widely proposals for a just income distribution can vary.

1. The question of income distribution is unimportant. Other values in life are more relevant than income.
2. Incomes should be derived only from work.
3. Complete equality of income modified by age, family size, etc.
4. The highest incomes (say the top 10 per cent) are too high.
5. The lowest incomes (say the lowest 10 per cent) are too low.
6. High and medium incomes are immoral as long as poverty exists.
7. Wage incomes should comprise a 'just' share of total income.
8. Progressive taxation.
9. Easily earned money ('windfalls') should be taxed at higher rates.
10. The income distribution should be 'fair' and should be based on a broad social consensus.
11. The income distribution should be allowed to develop from equal opportunity and in the absence of any discrimination.
12. To each according to his needs.
13. Priority for family needs.
14. Moral qualities of the services rendered should be reflected in income levels.
15. Leave the income distribution to market forces.

It is obvious that these different postulates cannot all be

combined. They are derived from different ethical and philosophical ideas and ideologies which allot different weights to different values (equality, effort, asceticism, tradition, etc.). For our purpose it is not necessary to analyse how different views of justice connect with these underlying ideologies, interesting as such an investigation might be. What matters is that the above list confirms what is recognizable in most discussions on distributional justice, namely that *on the whole* a majority of opinion tends to equate greater justice with a *movement* towards more income equality without, however, being definite or in agreement on the ultimate level of income differentiation to be desired. Among the various targets enumerated above, the norms numbered (2) to (9) and (13) clearly fall into this category, while the remaining norms betray no definite stand on this matter.

Without questioning the existence and the significance of the various norms, the above consideration probably justifies us in regarding a demand for a somewhat more equal distribution of incomes as a *general* ethical viewpoint where justice is concerned, and to confront this demand with the typical perspectives coming from economic quarters. Before dealing with the general aspects of this situation, I want to point out two cases where this ethical-economic confrontation has special significance: firstly, the position of utilitarianism with regard to income distribution and equalization demands and, secondly, the theory of justice put forward by the philosopher John Rawls.[3] Utilitarianism deserves special mention because of the dominant influence it had and still has on economic theory in general and on welfare economics in particular; and John Rawls is chosen from among many moral philosophers because his theory – being in closer touch with the economic problem than many others – found considerable sympathy among economic theorists.

As has been mentioned before, utilitarianism is a consequential ethical philosophy aiming at 'the greatest happiness of the greatest number' or, more prosaically, at 'maximum utility'. This provides a standard and a guide for action in welfare economics: measures which lead to an increase in utility are classified as desirable. Utilitarianism as such contains no 'rules' about distributional justice, nor can such rules be derived from its basic principles. If utility were measurable and comparable between different persons, then a distributional implication would be that income should be redistributed from persons with a low capacity to derive utility from their (marginal) income to persons with a high capacity. In this way the level of total utility – the 'sum of happiness' – could be increased. Depending on the initial situation, this 'rule' could mean an increase or a decrease of income inequality. In any case there is nothing which points towards income equality as a preferred position. If interpersonal comparisons of utility are not possible, we arrive at the New Welfare Economics which can still recommend pareto-superior constellations where some people are better off and nobody worse off than before. This will imply an increase in utility but can also result in greater or lesser income inequality. No valuations are possible at all when different Pareto-optimal positions are compared because this would require interpersonal comparisons of utility.

But this utilitarian indifference *vis-à-vis* judgements on income distribution disappears as soon as two simple assumptions are introduced. One argues that the fact that individual utilities are neither measurable nor observable does not preclude the fairly plausible assumption that capacities for deriving utility from income are normally distributed among persons, though we are not able to tell who has which capacity. The second assumption makes use of the 'economic law' of diminishing marginal utility of income. Adding these two assumptions to the basic utilitarian principle, one gets the result that income equality is an optimal utilitarian strategy for maximizing the *probability* of obtaining a high level of utility (which can be neither observed nor measured). This will now be shown for the case of two persons.

As a beginning we present in Figure 9.1 the case of two persons *A* and *B*, with identical utility functions in relation to income. We assume that a total income of £200 (depicted on the abscissa) is to be divided between *A* and *B*. On the ordinate we imagine the existence of a scale of (unobservable) marginal utilities. The curves *A'A"* and *B'B"* are the (unknown) marginal utility functions of *A* and *B*. (Total utilities are not shown in the diagram.) The sum accruing to *A* is measured from point *A* eastwards; the income of *B* is measured from point *B* westwards. Since we assume identical utility functions, the two curves are symmetrical mirror images. The total utility obtained by a person is given by the area under the marginal curve from the corresponding origin up to the point of the person's income. In the present example it is immediately obvious

Figure 9.1 *Utilitarian income distribution with homogeneous individuals*

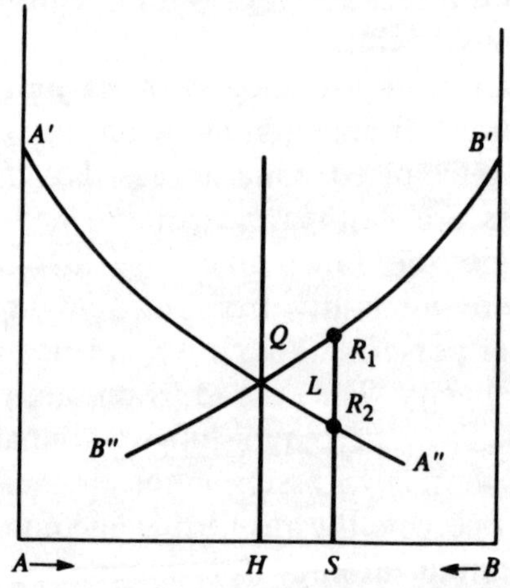

that an equal distribution of income in point *H* (with *A* and *B* each getting £100) will yield maximum utility. This is given by the area under the curve *AA'QB'B*. All other distributions lead to lower levels of aggregate utility. Taking, for example, the distribution in point *S* which favours *A*, we see that *A* obtains additional utility (over and above the equality position) of HQR_2S, while *B* suffers a loss of HQR_1 *S*. Added together this gives a net loss *L* (QR_1R_2), a consequence of the law of diminishing marginal utility: the gain from the transfer sum means less to *A* than the loss of an equal sum means to *B*.

In the trivial case of identical utility functions, income equality thus emerges quite clearly and unequivocally as an utilitarian optimum. But we must turn to the more realistic and relevant case where persons have different utility functions. This case is treated in Figure 9.2; this is identical with 9.1 except that *A* can derive higher utility

Figure 9.2 Utilitarian income distribution with heterogeneous individuals and uncertainty

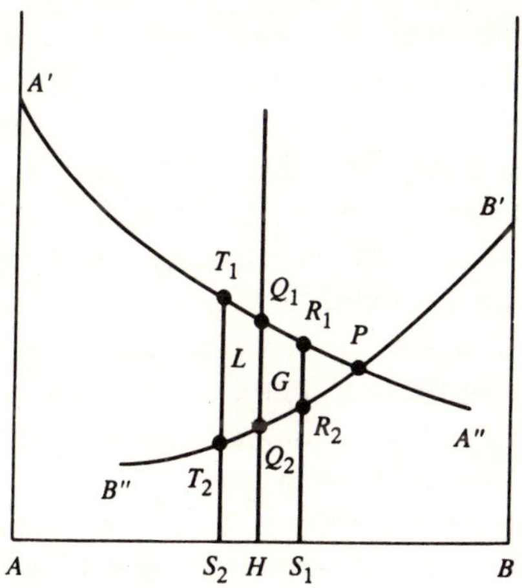

levels from a given income than B. If the utility functions of A and B were known, the point of maximum utility (the utilitarian optimum) could be established at the 'correct' point P where the two utility functions intersect. Income would be distributed unequally in favour of A who can 'produce' more utility. Total utility would reach a maximum of $AA'PB'B$.

But the positions of the utility curves are unknown. Thus it is quite possible that deviations from an equal distribution could lead to higher utility levels. But one has no idea whether to redistribute in favour of A or of B. If one goes in the 'right' direction – favouring A in our example (Figure 9.2) – the situation would be improved, but it gets worse when one moves in the opposite direction. The important point to note is that the effects of these two deviations are not symmetrical. Let us assume that one considers a redistribution through deviating from the equality position by an amount of HS which can go either to A (HS_1) or to B (HS_2). In the first case, a net gain of utility $G = Q_2Q_1R_1R_2$ is achieved; in the second case a net loss $L = Q_1T_1T_2Q_2$. The different positions of the two utility curves in combination with diminishing marginal utility will then always cause L to be greater than G. This is so because the utility which A gains when favoured weighs less than the loss of the same sum when he is the loser; this effect cannot be compensated by reactions in the opposite direction in B's utility calculus which follows analogous rules. Of course the same is true (i.e. $L > G$) when we assume that B has a higher capacity for deriving utility from income. This probability of getting less utility rather than more when deviating from an equal income distribution (without information about the utility functions) makes it possible to regard income equality as an optimal solution from a utilitarian standpoint.

Next we turn to the ethical ideas of Rawls. Rawls's *Theory of Justice* is a wide-ranging important work which touches upon a great number of philosophical and moral issues. We restrict ourselves here to a short summary of those points which have a direct bearing on our problem. Rawls's ideas are in the utilitarian tradition since he accepts that increases in individual utility are a desirable welfare target. What he misses in the utilitarian concept is a rule about justice which would enable us to move beyond the Pareto-optimum rule and provide a standard for choosing a 'just' income distribution.

In his search for a criterion of justice, Rawls follows the tradition of classical political philosophy to derive rules for a 'just' order of society from a hypothetical 'social contract' on which all rational individuals could agree in a pre-societal 'original position'.[4] Rawls chooses this method and looks for the principles on which a community of people could (or should?) agree unanimously if decisions had to be made 'under a veil of ignorance'. By this is meant that no person would know which position they would have in the chosen system, whether they would be rich or poor, educated or not, upper class or lower class, etc.

Under these circumstances – according to his argument – an 'equity' ideal would find general consensus, taking a different form on each of two different levels. A first level (which will not occupy us in what follows) covers all aspects of individual freedom; in this sphere the highest possible degree of freedom is to be aimed at as long as no freedom rights of other persons are violated. On this level absolute equality is the rule: all people should have equal access to all rights of freedom.

On the second level which deals with 'our' problem – the just distribution of material goods – Rawls does not stipulate perfect equality as the consensus solution. He introduces a 'difference principle' which takes into account that the level of total output (and with it the level of utility attainable) is not independent of income structures. With incomes differentiated according to talent and efficiency, such a relationship is assumed. But what should be the degree of 'just' differentiation which could find general acceptance under a veil of ignorance? Rawls's answer is that income inequalities or changes in income structures should be admitted (regarded as 'better') if, in the chosen situation, the income[5] of *the least advantaged persons* is improved (or maximized) in comparison with existing alternatives. Rawls expects that such a rule would be accepted as a general target because of the widespread existence of risk aversion. People who cannot foresee their future position would vote for such a rule because it carries a guarantee that they will obtain special consideration if they are *very* badly off.

Before I give some illustrations of the distributional effects of this rule, I want to say a few words about the reasons which have created a special interest for Rawls's theory among economists (insofar as they are prepared to be interested in 'justice'). After all Rawls was not the first or only moral philosopher with ideas about distributional justice. Both before and after him other ideas have also been presented. That his assumptions are not the only basis for a solution was amply proved by the discussions which followed his publication and which suggested several modifications and alternatives. But what makes Rawls particularly attractive to economists is that – in contrast to most other philosophers – his argumentation includes elements which are closely related to concepts already used in economic theory, making them relevant for a concept of 'justice'. Two elements are of particular importance: (1) the explicit acknowledgement of the role which income levels and income differences can play in motivation and allocation, and thus for efficiency and output levels, and (2) the special and by no means self-evident assumption of strict risk-aversion behaviour in the form of a maximin strategy which tries to avoid 'worst cases' – an assumption contained in game theory with which economists are familiar.

Let us return to Rawls's theory and to an illustration of his rule for justice. It is obvious that every Pareto-optimal improvement will also be acceptable to Rawls.[6] But the important point is that his rule permits an ordering between alternative Pareto-optima and offers a special menu of priorities. The following simple numerical example of alternative income distributions can serve as an illustration.

	A	*B*	*C*	*Y*
(1)	100	60	40	200
(2)	120	80	41	241
(3)	90	60	42	192

A, *B* and *C* represent three persons or three homogeneous groups of equal size. The columns contain their production and income positions in three alternative situations numbered 1 to 3. *Y* represents total real income in each situation. When situations (1) and (2) are compared, (2) presents an 'improvement' both on the Pareto and Rawls criterion. Everyone is better off than in (1), including the least advantaged group *C*. Note, however, that (2) displays a higher degree of income differentiation than (1). This is accepted by Rawls because group *C* benefits from this increase in inequality. If we include situation (3) in our consideration, in which a redistribution from rich to poor causes a reduction in output, we find that on Rawls's terms, this lower and less differentiated income distribution dominates constellations (1) and (2) because group *C* is better off under these conditions. When Pareto criteria are taken as a standard, then a change from (1) or (2) to (3) can neither be recommended nor rejected; in both cases there are winners and losers.

As we can see, neither the utilitarian approach nor the Rawls rules equate justice and equality of incomes. But both indicate a presumption that movements in the direction of more, though not necessarily complete, equality are likely to lead to a better approximation of the chosen norms of justice. They therefore fit into the general picture which shows that most ethical approaches usually favour more income equality. Economists on the other hand, with efficiency as their main desideratum, tend to take a sceptical or even hostile view regarding demands for income levelling.

Insofar as there is a trade-off between justice and efficiency, the question of which 'mixture' should become practical policy can only be decided in a broad political process. Neither the one side, the 'moralists', nor the other, the economists, are entitled to a special position as experts who can decide which way should be taken. Their views are of course important and can be improved when moralists acquire some insights about economic processes so as to avoid utopian elements in their demands,[7] and when economists try to free themselves from too strict an adherence to the structures of their rigid theoretical models. The ethics versus efficiency conflict cannot be treated on a 'purely objective' basis separated from the broader socio-political debate, although the main elements involved in this conflict can be presented analytically. This will now be done with the hope of gaining a more concentrated picture of some of the points discussed so far.[8]

We begin with the simplest case when an already existing quantity of goods (real income) has to be distributed. After that we shall advance to the critical case where output has yet to be produced, a production not independent of the way output (income) is distributed. Figure 9.3 presents an Edgeworth box[9] with two persons, A and *B*, and two goods, *X* and *Y*, which are measured along the two axes. *X* and *Y* are to be divided up between *A* and *B*. Here no efficiency problem arises since the income to be shared already exists. One can therefore simply follow an ethical recommendation for income equality which in the present example means that both *A* and *B* get half the amount of the given *X* and *Y*. This distribution is shown by *P* in the diagram. If no other considerations play a role, this distribution will also be regarded as 'fair' which is a special notion of justice to be discussed later on. It is not difficult to see that *P* meets the Rawls criterion: every distribution

Figure 9.3 Income equality modified by Pareto-optimality

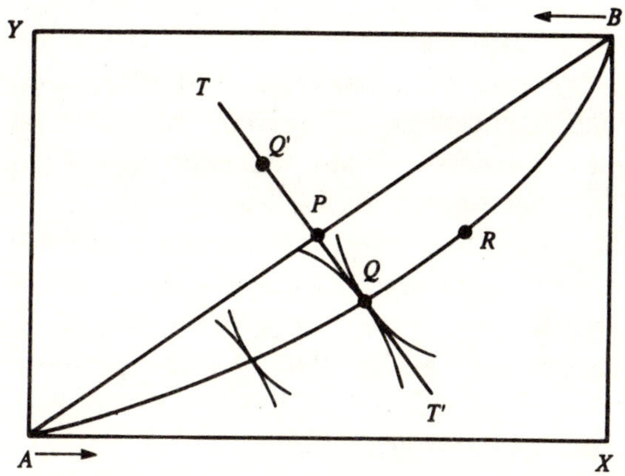

which deviates from P would demand a redistribution in favour of the person who is worse off than the other person, a process which would continue until one landed at P. Then no further Rawls improvement would be possible.

As long as A and B have identical utility functions, P is also a Pareto-optimal position. If, however, their preferences differ so that A has a stronger preference for X or Y than B, then – when markets are given – both persons can improve their position through an exchange of goods. Let TT' in Figure 9.3 be the exchange relation between X and Y which the 'free market' establishes.[10] The exchange process will then lead to an 'equilibrium' in point Q which lies on the contract curve $AQRB$. This distribution is now Pareto-optimal and could be called 'income equality modified by Pareto-optimality'.

Two characteristics of the constellation Q should be noted. The first refers to the fact that Q is not necessarily a utilitarian optimum. It is the Pareto-optimum which can be reached (through exchange) from an initial income equality, but it is not the Pareto-optimum which maximizes the (unknown) total utility. If *A* has a greater capacity for utility creation than *B*, then the point of 'maximum utility' could, for instance, be *R*. To get there by a process of exchange one would have to start from an initial position of unequal incomes. The second characteristic concerns the idea of 'fairness'. Given the exchange relation in Figure 9.3, we see that *A* and *B* cannot only reach point *Q* but could also move to *Q′* where their positions (regarding possessions of *X* and *Y*) are exactly reversed. As *A*'s and *B*'s indifference curves show, neither of them would prefer *Q′* to *Q*. That means that *Q* is a 'fair' solution if a fair distribution is defined as one which involves no envy by any individual of any other.[11]

We can now turn to the truly problematic case where income distribution has an effect on the level of production. But once again it must be stressed that we are dealing with only a segment of the distribution problem where ethics (more equality) and economics (more output) come into conflict. The existence of conditions where these two targets supplement each other – at least up to a certain point – should not be overlooked. Apart from the already mentioned possibility of productivity gains connected with higher incomes for the poor, this will particularly be the case if redistribution affects the 'rents' of monopolistic activities which lie above the necessary incentive payments or when preferences for real income are very high among taxed persons so that reductions in their net incomes will induce them to increase their efforts rather than reduce them.

The 'dilemma model' to which we now turn consists of two persons: a highly qualified *A* and a less qualified *B*. *A* can earn a higher wage than *B* and in both cases wage levels influence the supply of effort. Redistribution takes place exclusively by levying a proportional tax on the higher wage and using the proceeds as a transfer payment to *B*.

We start our diagrammatical analysis with a description of *A*'s behaviour. In Figure 9.4 *T* represents time over which *A* can dispose; it is measured along the abscissa. On the ordinate we have real income *X*. In each period (day, week . . .) *A* has a total of OB_1 hours at his disposal which he can divide up between paid work and 'leisure'. Leisure and income are both sources of utility (the utility function is $U = U(X, T)$ with *T* for leisure time). Between income and leisure we have a trade-off, with utility maximization determining their combination. The trade-off between leisure time *given up*, which is measured on the abscissa moving from B_1 in the direction of the origin, and the (real) income which can be obtained for it depends on the (real) wage per unit of time (hourly wages). The size of the wage (in terms of *X*) is given by the slope of the line

Figure 9.4 The choice between work and leisure: effects of a wage tax (1)

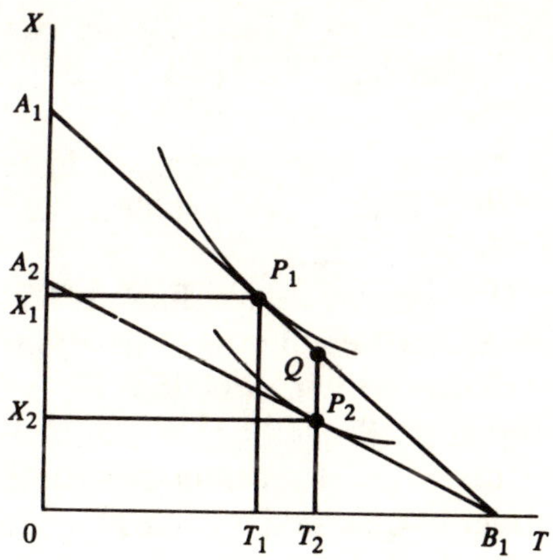

B_1A_1.The greater the slope the higher the income which can be earned per hour. If A would give up his total time budget for paid (market) work, he could earn a maximal income of OA_1. The utility function $U(X, T)$ is indicated by two indifference curves in Figure 9.4. If the wage is given by B_1A_1 we obtain maximum utility in P_1: B_1T_1 hours will be supplied on the labour market in order to obtain an income of OX_1. The combination of income X_1 and leisure time T_1 (both measured from the origin) represents the optimal decision of the neoclassical 'homo oeconomicus'.

Let us assume that a proportional tax is imposed on A's income. His net income will then fall by a certain proportion. This is illustrated in Figure 9.4 by the net wage line B_1A_2. The higher the tax rate the greater will be the angle between the gross and net wage line. If the utility function takes the form we have given it in 9.4, then A will move from P_1 to P_2 after the tax has been introduced. This means that he reduces his labour supply and expands his leisure time (whose 'opportunity costs' in terms of income lost has fallen) by T_1T_2, thereby reducing his net income by X_1X_2 (with gross income equal to T_2Q). The new optimal combination is X_2 and T_2 and corresponds to the assumption that income and leisure are normal substitutional goods. The reduction of the net wage means that real income has become 'more expensive' in terms of leisure time so less of it is demanded (unless the demand for income is perfectly inelastic).

From Figure 9.4 we can derive Figure 9.5. Gross and net wage lines and the 'equilibrium' positions P_1 and P_2 are taken over from 9.4. In addition we have a curve $P_1P_2B_1$ which contains all equilibrium positions connected with alternative tax rates. It is obtained by moving B_1A_1 continually counter-clockwise and marking the points of tangency with the indifference curves. As tax rates rise, the supply of labour shrinks continuously until it disappears altogether when the tax rate reaches 100 per cent. For

Figure 9.5 *The choice between work and leisure: effects of a wage tax (2)*

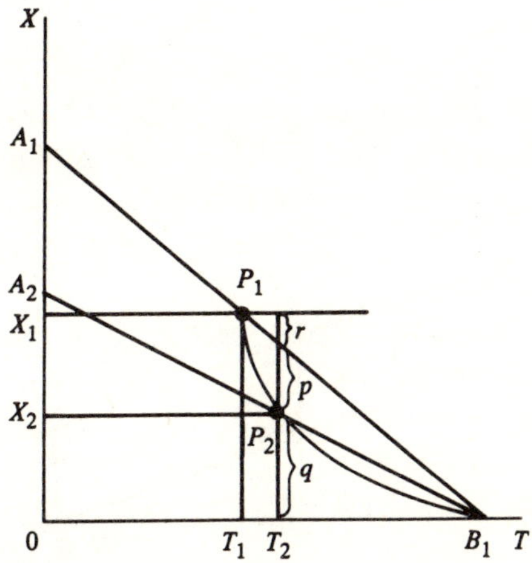

each tax rate we can read three elements from the diagram. They are shown for the situation P_2 by q, p and r. At the given tax rate the gross income of A falls by r (because of his reduced working time) and out of this income a tax p has to be paid so that A is left with a net income of q.[12]

Next we turn to Figure 9.6 which deals with B's behaviour. To make a distinction *vis-à-vis* A we denote B's income by Y. As B's wage rate is lower than A's, the wage line B_1A_1 is less steep than the corresponding line in Figure 9.4. When B obtains a fixed transfer income Tr (equal to the tax revenue obtained from A), her work income will be increased by exactly this sum independently of the amount of work she is doing. This is shown in the diagram by a parallel to the wage line lying above it by a distance equal to Tr. With B's utility function as given in the diagram, this transfer leads to a shift of her optimum position from P_1 to P_2 (or from Y_1, T_1 to Y_2, T_2). This means that

Figure 9.6 The choice between work and leisure: effects of transfer payments (1)

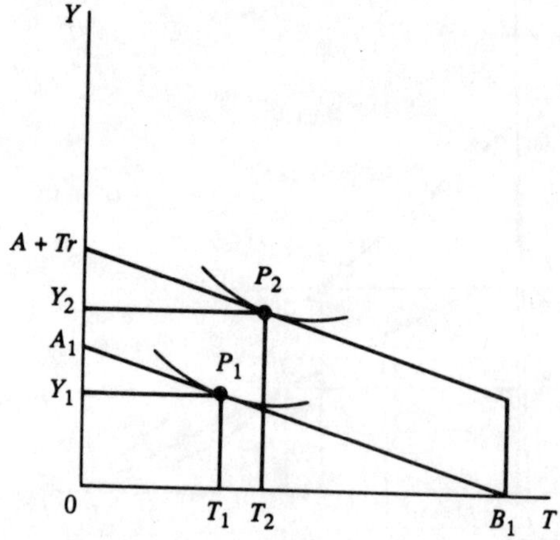

B now enjoys more income and more leisure time. This again points to the 'normality' of the two goods: the improved budget condition after the transfer has taken place leads to an increase in demand for both competing goods – income and leisure.

Just as we derived Figure 9.5 from Figure 9.4, we can obtain Figure 9.7 from 9.6. The wage line B_1A_1 and the equilibrium positions P_1 and P_2 are directly transferred from 9.6. By varying the transfer sum we get for every parallel to the wage line a point of tangency with an indifference curve indicating the corresponding equilibrium. The curve running from P_1 through P_2 in Figure 9.7 is the locus of all these equilibrium points. The curve shows how income and leisure grow in spite of reduced efforts when transfer incomes are increased. In a given situation, say P_2, work income is lower by *s* than it would be without redistribution, but total available income is higher by *t*.

Figure 9.7 The choice between work and leisure: effects of transfer payments (2)

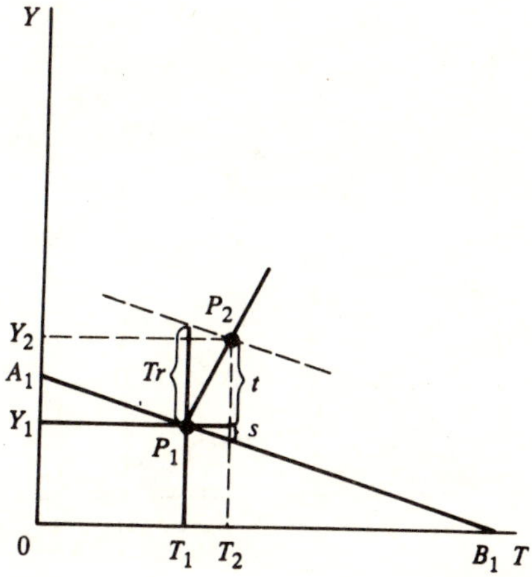

Figures 9.5 and 9.7 can now be used to present in a slightly changed form the relationships between gross and net incomes (after taxes and transfers). This will make the ensuing diagrammatic analysis of the total situation more manageable. Figure 9.8, which is derived from 9.5, shows for *A* the relation between gross income X^g (measured along the ordinate) and available net income X^n (on the abscissa) for alternative tax rates (not shown in the diagram). At X_1 we have a state where no tax is levied: $X^g = X^n$. X_1' lies on the 45° line indicating the equality of gross and net income. When taxes are introduced, net income falls (i.e. X^n moves towards the origin) for two reasons: (1) because *A* works less than before, and (2) he must pay a tax. Since gross income is only affected by the first factor, it falls less than net income. Tax revenue p first rises and then falls as tax rates rise until we get $X^g = X^n = p = 0$ at a tax rate of 100 per cent. These relation-

Figure 9.8 Relationships between gross and net incomes for A

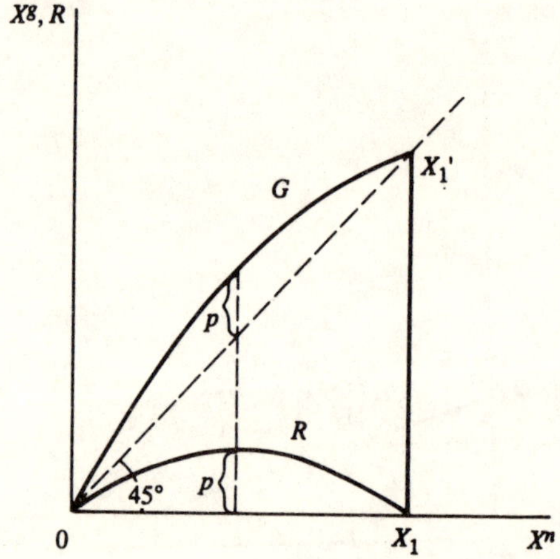

ships are summarized in Figure 9.8 where the curves *G* and *R* and the corresponding point on the abscissa give us readings of gross income, tax revenue and available net income respectively for alternative tax rates (zero in X_1 and 100 per cent at the origin).

In an analogous way we derive for *B* Figure 9.9 from 9.7. The influence of alternative transfer incomes on working time and work income *W* and on the available total income Y^n $(W + Tr)$ is shown by the curves *W* and Y^n. As the transfer sums (measured along the abscissa and transposed through the 45°-line to the ordinate) increase, the labour input declines; total income increases, though less than the increase in transfer payments.

Figures 9.8 and 9.9 form the basis for the total model contained in Figures 9.10 and 9.11. In Figure 9.10 the first quadrant shows the relationship between transfer and *B*'s total income (derived from 9.9) and the second quadrant

Figure 9.9 Relationships between gross and net incomes for B

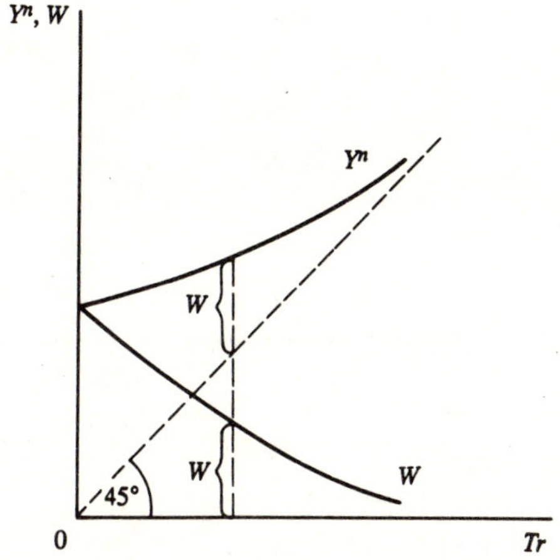

that between tax revenue and A's net income (from 9.8). The third quadrant only serves for transferring X^n values from the abscissa to the ordinate so that we obtain in quadrant four the distributional relationship which is the object of our analysis – the combinations of X^n and Y^n which result from alternative tax rates (redistributions) when their effects on incentives are taken into account. The 'tax-free' initial position is given by X_1 and Y_1 pictured as the distribution P_1 in the fourth quadrant. Let us now assume that a tax rate of a given size is imposed on A's wage. As a consequence his net income falls (less work plus tax deduction) let us say to X_2. From the R-curve in the second quadrant we can read off the resulting tax revenue p which as transfer determines B's adjustment and total income, which is given as Y_2 by the Y^n curve in the first quadrant. X_2 and the corresponding Y_2 present the new distributional situation which is shown by P_2 in the

Figure 9.10 A model of the justice–efficiency dilemma

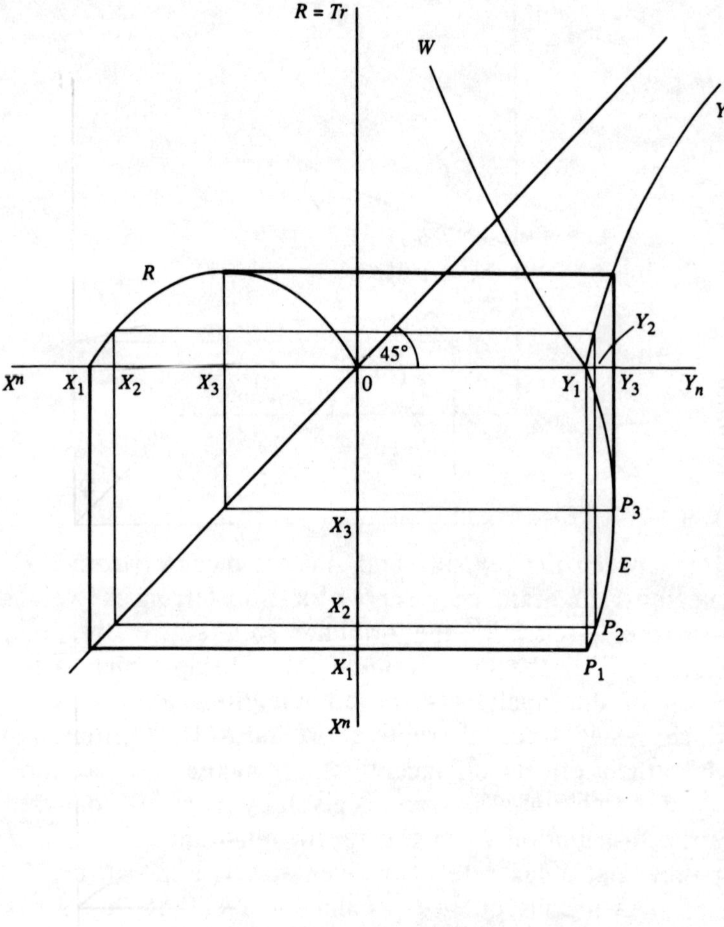

Figure 9.11 Two varieties of the justice–efficiency dilemma

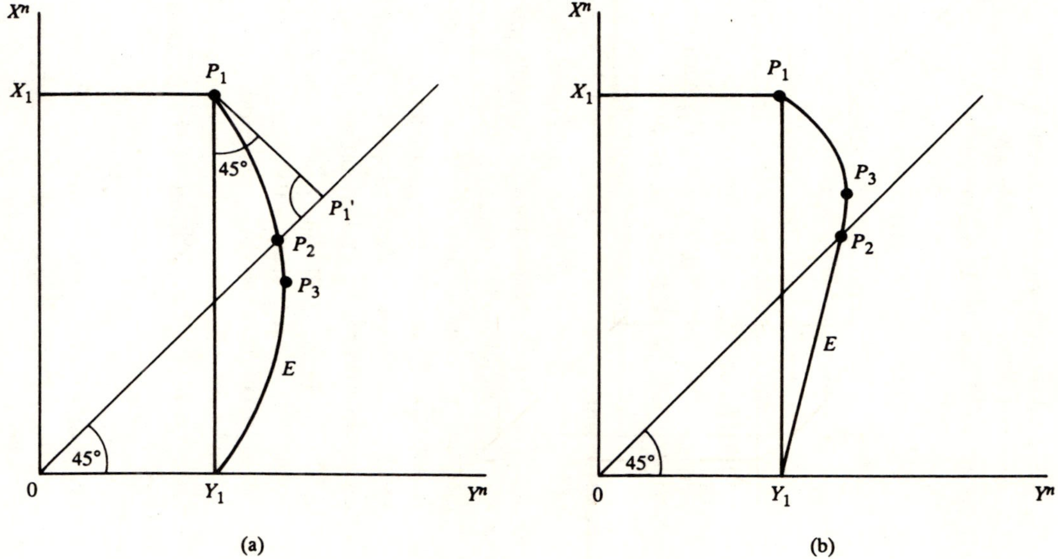

fourth quadrant. Analogous relations are obtained for other tax rates. Maximal redistribution naturally occurs when the tax revenue, and with it the transfer, reach their highest value. This is given by X_3, Y_3 and P_3. Finally, the *E*-curve in the fourth quadrant is the locus of all 'equilibrium' distributions resulting from different tax rates imposed on *A*. *A*'s income can vary between X_1 and zero; *B*'s income never falls below Y_1 (because she is not taxed by assumption) and lies above Y_1 when redistribution takes place.

Figures 9.11(a) and (b) concentrate on the final picture of the distributional alternatives of the fourth quadrant of 9.10. They show the ultimate available incomes of *A* and *B*, i.e. X^n and Y^n. The diagrams are a 'magnified' version of the fourth quadrant of Figure 9.10 with the X^n axis turned upward. Added to this is the 45° line as the locus of all distributions where final incomes are equal ($X^n = Y^n$). In 9.11(a) the point P_1 (X_1, Y_1) represents the position where no tax is in force. *A* is better off than *B*. If the total product to be shared were fixed, income could be redistributed along the line P_1P_1': what is taken from *A* would accrue fully to *B*. 'Ethical' equality could be reached in P_1'. But when redistribution affects labour input and production negatively, taxation leads to a loss in macroeconomic 'efficiency' and we can no longer move along P_1P_1'; we are restricted to a path along the *E*-curve. From a purely 'economic' point of view, this by itself can be taken as an argument against redistribution. The reduction in output is 'bad'. If on the other hand an extreme 'ethical' principle of absolute equality were adopted, one would move – through taxes and transfers – to point P_2. This 'solution' would also agree with the Rawls-principle because up to P_2 the position of the person most badly off is improved.

However, the principle of absolute equality and the Rawls-principle need not coincide. This is shown in 9.11(b) where the *E*-curve has a slightly different shape (following from different intensities in the behaviour patterns of *A* and *B*). In this case the equality rule would dictate a move to P_2 while Rawls would stop short at P_3 because the position of the 'poorest' person (B) is only improved up to this point and not beyond it. At P_3 the income distribution is still unequal – *A* is better off than *B* – but a further redistribution would reduce efficiency so much that, though *B* would still gain relatively, she would be worse off in absolute terms compared with P_3.[13]

In addition to the idea of 'justice' as an ethical category which can come into conflict with economic ideologies when questions of income distribution are discussed, we have another category with ethical undertones which is not unimportant in this field. It is the idea of 'fairness', of a 'fair distribution', whose normative conceptions often play an important role in actual disputes (such as the demand for 'fair wages'). Justice and fairness are both moral categories. But they differ in two respects when questions of income distribution are considered. One difference concerns the 'status' of the two principles: justice is 'hierarchically' on a higher plane than fairness. The search for justice is based on a philosophical attempt to find absolute principles which – if possible – should have universal validity irrespective of time and place. Fairness on the other hand rests on rules of conduct which are supported by a broad social consensus but do not claim to deserve acceptance *sub auspicie aeternitatis*. The second difference is one of stress as far as contents are concerned. The idea of justice normally (though not necessarily) starts from the individual, his or her needs, rights, duties, etc. which should be preserved in a just order. Fairness on the other hand looks from the very beginning on the relative position of people in a societal setting. Absolute levels are only of secondary importance.

Fairness and distribution therefore need some additional considerations when we deal with the confrontation of ethical and economic valuations.[14] In order to do this we must – as in the case of justice – accept some criterion for fairness which can be regarded as widely acceptable, even though fairness tends to be a vague notion which can be interpreted in several different ways. One widely acceptable general definition regards a distribution as fair if it provokes no envy by any individual of any other; in our case, this must be understood as absence of envy with regard to real income in a wide sense, including the type and amount of work that must be input to obtain the given money income. We shall use this definition of fairness in the following considerations.

When we are dealing with the distribution of a fixed amount, then by definition equal shares are always a fair solution. Nobody will have a reason to envy somebody else's position. If the equal shares consist of a basket of different goods and if the persons have different preferences, the position of all can be improved through exchange. The new position so achieved – 'income equality modified by Pareto-optimality' (see p. 133) – is also fair since after the exchange each person will prefer the new combination of goods to the bundle which he/she has given up: no envy will arise. This case has already been considered for the two-person two-goods model on p. 132–3.

Though equal shares (as an initial condition) will always be a fair solution, it is not the only one. Initial inequality can also be regarded as fair by all participants when goods and tastes are not homogeneous. This can be shown very simply in a two-person example. Between two persons, *A* and *B*, a cake is to be divided, two-thirds of which is filled with sultanas (*S*) and one-third with nuts (*N*) in a way which is illustrated in Figure 9.12. A good rule for a fair division between two persons says that one person should determine the partition and the other person be allowed to choose which part he or she wants. If *A* cuts the cake across the middle as shown in 9.12(a), a fair solution is guaranteed. But if *A* prefers sultanas and at the same time knows that *B* very much prefers nuts, then he could decide to cut the cake along the lines shown in 9.12(b). *B* will

Figure 9.12 Alternative examples of fair distributions

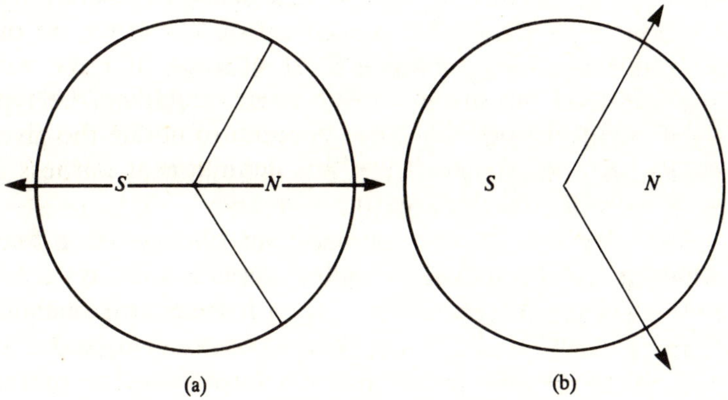

then choose the N-part of the cake, being content with one-third of the cake, while A will obtain two-thirds. This (initial) distribution turns out to be unequal but fair; neither of the two persons would like to change positions with the other. Baumol calls such a situation where each person receives a bundle which is *strictly* preferred by that individual to the bundle received by anyone else (i.e. if his or her holdings could be reduced somewhat without giving rise to envy) 'superfairness'. This simple example shows that – just as with Pareto-optimality – several 'competing' solutions can exist which all meet our chosen fairness criterion. Furthermore, as will be shown below, fairness solutions do not necessarily coincide with Pareto-optimality. Some pareto-inferior distributions may be regarded as fairer than better allocations to all participants if they permit an 'envy-free' relationship between the various incomes.

Once again we can summarize our arguments analytically

taking the case of two persons. *A* and *B*, between whom two given goods, *X* and *Y*, are to be distributed in a 'fair' way. Figure 9.13 presents an Edgeworth box which, however, in this case is used for a special discussion of *A*'s position alone. The indifference curves I_1I_1 and I_2I_2 are two samples from *A*'s preference function for *X* and *Y*. These two indifference curves are mirrored in $I_1'I_1'$ and $I_2'I_2'$. In other words, these two latter curves are exactly equal to I_1I_1 and I_2I_2, the only difference being that they are related to 0_2 as origin instead of 0_1. Both types of indifference curves represent *A*'s preferences but are measured from different origins. Corresponding dashed and undashed curves always cut each other in two points, for instance, *P* and *P'* or *Q* and *Q'*. Let us now look at a distribution in *P* under the assumption that *A*'s share is measured from 0_1 and *B*'s from 0_2. A obtains 0_1X_1 of *X* and 0_1Y_1 of *Y*; *B*'s amounts are consequently 0_2X_2 and 0_2Y_2. Seen from

Figure 9.13 Fair distributions

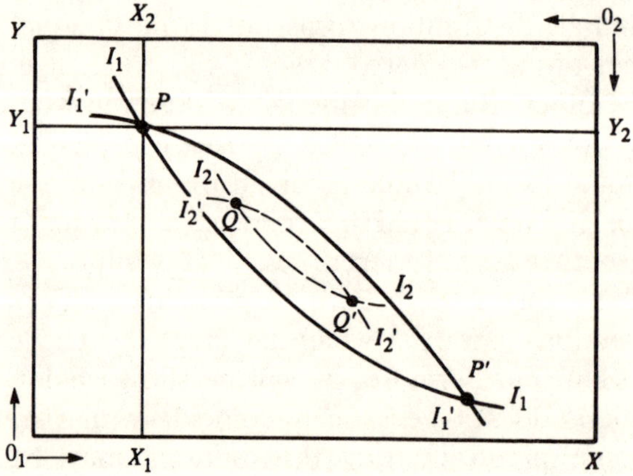

A's perspective these two shares are 'equivalent' since *A* is indifferent between them; they lie on the same indifference curve, once measured from 0_1 (I_1I_1) and once from 0_2 ($I_1'I_1'$). *P* therefore represents a 'fair' distribution as far as *A* is concerned: he can feel no envy for *B*'s bundle.

What has been shown for *P* is equally valid for all other intersections of corresponding indifference curves, such as *P'*, *Q*, *Q'* etc. When all these points are joined we obtain *A*'s 'fairness curve' which is shown in the Edgeworth box of Figure 9.14 (now valid in the normal way for *A* and *B*) as the curve F_1F_1. All distributions on this curve will be regarded as fair by *A*. Distributions to the south-west of F_1F_1 will be felt as unfair (in our definition) because then *A* would 'envy' *B*: he would prefer to have *B*'s bundle of goods rather than his own. In an analogous way to F_1F_1 we can derive a fairness curve for *B* which in 9.14 is given by F_2F_2. All distributions north-east of F_2F_2 are unfair as far as *B* is concerned.

Before proceeding to an interpretation of this fairness

Figure 9.14 Fairness curves

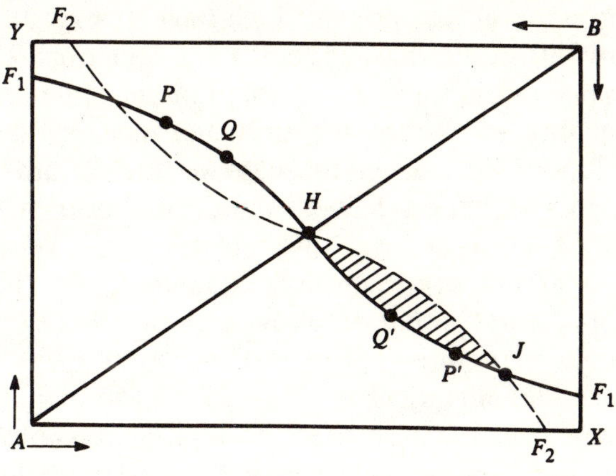

'model', three characteristics of fairness curves should be noted. The first concerns point H in 9.14. This is the point of equal shares and as such must lie on *every* fairness curve because no envy for the other person's bundle can arise.[15] Secondly it can be shown that the two branches of the fairness curve extending from H are symmetrical *vis-à-vis* the diagonal. Taking for instance the positions P and P' in 9.13, which lie on the same indifference curve (of A), we can see that A obtains (measured from 0_1) in P the combination X_1 and Y_1 and in P' the combination $(X - X_1)$, $(Y - Y_1)$. The two are symmetrical in relation to H. A third and final observation tells us that A's and B's fairness curves will coincide when their preferences are identical. This, too, can easily be derived from Figure 9.13. There I_1I_1 is an indifference curve of A as seen from 0_1 and $I_1'I_1'$ a transfer of the same curve to 0_2 as the origin. Since B's indifference curves are related to 0_2, identity of preferences will mean that $I_1'I_1'$ is an indifference curve of B corresponding exactly to A's I_1I_1 which in turn becomes B's transfer curve for $I_1'I_1'$ with P and P' as points of intersection. P and P' and equally Q and Q' and so on therefore belong to the fairness curve of both A and B.

We can now summarize the results of our analysis, touching upon all the points which have emerged so far. A first obvious result has already been mentioned twice: equal shares are always a fair solution: no envy can arise. But equality is neither the only nor necessarily the optimal solution. Just as in the case of the Pareto-criterion, the fairness-criterion delivers a multitude of possible 'solutions' which lie on or 'over' the fairness curves of A and B. The only argument for absolute equality consists in the fact that it is *always* a fair solution and can therefore serve as a minimal requirement or starting point. Only when preferences are identical is an equal distribution also the optimum because it secures the highest possible utility levels for both participants (on the indifference curves passing through H). When preferences differ, 'superfair' solutions are possible which can provide more utility than the equality principle. This was shown in our earlier example of the cake. The general case is indicated in Figure 9.14 where every distribution within the shaded area between *H* and *J* is preferable for both participants compared to their minimal demands regarding fairness.

Finally the important point has to be made that fair distributions do not necessarily coincide with a Pareto-optimum. As an example take Figure 9.15. F_1F_1 and F_2F_2 are the fairness curves of *A* and *B*. *P′* presents quite clearly a fair distribution: it lies on *A*'s and above *B*'s fairness curve. If *A*'s and *B*'s preferences have the form as illustrated by the indifference curves I_1I_1 and $I_2I_2(I_2'I_2')$ respectively, then *P′* is not a Pareto-optimum. A distribution in *R* would improve *B*'s position (shift from I_2I_2 to $I_2'I_2'$) without affecting *A*'s utility who continues to stay on the same difference curve. But *R* lies below *A*'s fairness curve and is therefore – in contrast to *P′* – unacceptable to him

Figure 9.15 Fairness and Pareto-optimality

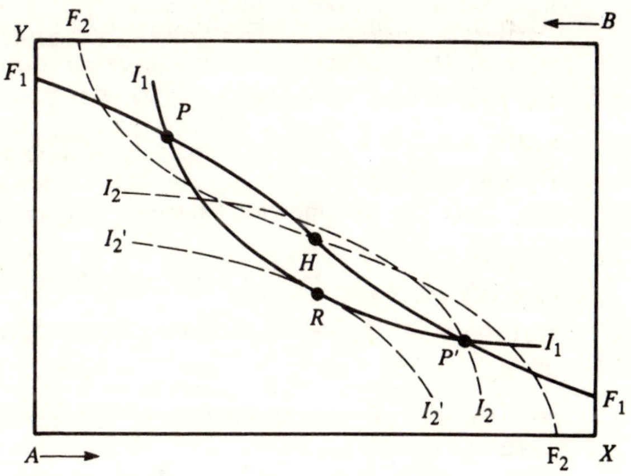

because it is 'unfair'. Thus while R dominates P' on Pareto-criteria, it is dominated by P' on fairness principles. The apparent contradiction that R and P' lie on the same indifference curve (of A) and yet P' is preferred is easily dissolved. The indifference curve tells us something about the valuation of goods in isolation; the fairness curve includes considerations about the possessions of other persons – whether I can regard them without 'envy' or not.

Fairness as an ethical category can form a bridge between justice and efficiency insofar as some deviations from a rigid ideal of justice might be accepted – traditionally and institutionally – as 'fair' and this could provide more flexibility for achieving desirable incentive and allocation effects. But the basic conflict between ethical and economic values and ideologies can only be smoothed in this way; it cannot be removed altogether. Discussions about 'trade-offs' between conflicting perspectives are bound to continue: they are a never-ending story.

Notes

1. These five targets formed the frequently quoted 'magic pentagon'. A reduced version was the 'magic triangle' covering only full employment, price stability and balance of payments equilibrium (or alternatively economic growth). In later years and particularly after the 'conservative turn-about' in the 1970s, the magic polygons were relegated to the background. Targets were now defined more narrowly, with price stability in the foreground and – closely connected with it – demands for balanced budgets and reduced state activity.
2. J. Pen (1971), *Income Distribution*, London: Allen Lane, The Penguin Press.
3. J. Rawls (1971), *A Theory of Justice*, Cambridge, Mass.: Harvard University Press.
4. Among the most prominent classical representatives of this approach we find Thomas Hobbes, John Locke and Jean-Jacques Rousseau.
5. Income is to be understood in a wide sense: wage income, profits, transfer incomes, social services, etc. The concept of justice and just distributions can easily be fitted into discussions about the welfare state.

6. If a certain Pareto-optimal change does not improve the situation of the least advantaged group (but must, of course, not deteriorate it according to the rules of the game!), the change will still be acceptable to Rawls as long as some intermediate income group benefits and the income chances of the lower groups are not threatened.
7. This does not mean that utopias may not be useful as an intellectual aid in thinking about long-term developments.
8. The following analysis is based on a paper by G. Gabisch, 'Konzepte und Implikationen der Gleichverteilung' (Concepts and implications of equality of incomes) in H. Hesse (ed.), *Wirtschaftswissenschaften und Ethik* (Economic Theory and Ethics), Berlin: Duncker & Humblot, 1988, pp. 71–84.
9. On the Edgeworth-box see p. 60.
10. To obtain a *determinate* exchange relation (price relation) we have to go beyond the two-person case and assume free and perfect atomic competition. In the two-person case, other elements are also at work like bargaining power and bargaining skills.
11. The question of fairness is treated on pp. 145–52.
12. As the diagram shows, the tax revenue (p) will – with a rising tax rate – at first rise and then fall because of reduced working time. The shape of this curve $P_1P_2B_1$ corresponds to the so-called 'Laffer curve'.
13. It must be stressed that the discussion in this chapter concentrates exclusively on the question of *income* levels and distributions. If the ideals of justice are directed at levels and distributions of *utility* (however ascertained), then an optimum solution need not involve income equality (moderate of absolute) as a target. Other factors, in particular the equality and status of the work supplied (its utility or disutility), have also to be considered. But these and other elements (e.g. age, health, family size, etc.) can be objectively ascertained and taken into account in distributional decisions without invalidating the basic idea of income equality.
14. With regard to the following see H. R. Varian (1975), 'Distributive justice, welfare economics, and the theory of fairness', *Philosophy and Public Affairs,* **4**, Spring; W. J. Baumol (1982), 'Applied fairness theory and rationing policy', *American Economic Review,* **72** (4), September.
15. That H is part of the fairness curve also follows from the way it is constructed. Remembering the derivation of the fairness curve in Figure 9.13, it is obvious that the point H, with $X_1 = X/2$ and $Y_1 = Y/2$, must lie on I_H, I_H *and* on I'_H I'_H. It is its own mirror point.

Further Reading

The literature dealing with the subject and the themes of this book has expanded considerably over the years. Even a moderately full bibliography would fill many pages. Instead of making an incomplete attempt in this direction, I restrict myself to name only a few works (in addition to those quoted in the text) which in my opinion can help the interested reader to delve deeper into the questions and problems raised in this short treatise. Most of the books mentioned contain useful bibliographies which give access to still wider studies.

On the subject in general and the aspects treated in Chapter 2, the following books (among others) deserve attention: A. K. Sen (1987), *On Ethics and Economics*, Oxford: Blackwell; E. F. Paul, J. Paul and F. D. Miller eds. (1985), *Ethics and Economics*, Oxford: Blackwell; H. Hesse ed. (1988), *Wirtschaftswissenschaften und Ethik*, Berlin: Duncker und Humblot.

On Chapter 1:

Plamenatz, J. (1970), *The English Utilitarians*, Oxford: Blackwell.

Sprigge, T. L. S. (1988), *The Rational Foundations of Ethics*, London: Routledge.

On Chapter 3:

Boland, L. A. (1982), *The Foundations of Economic Method*, London: Allen and Unwin.

Myrdal, G. (1958), *Value in Social Theory. A Selection of Essays in Methodology* (edited by Paul Streeten), London: Routledge and Kegan Paul.

On Chapter 4:

Elster, J. (1989), *The Cement of Society*, Cambridge: Cambridge University Press.

On Chapter 5:

Buchanan, A. (1985), *Ethics, Efficiency and the Market*, Oxford: Clarendon.

On Chapter 6:

Graaf, J. de V. (1957), *Theoretical Welfare Economics*, Cambridge: Cambridge University Press.

Little, I. M. D. (1950), *A Critique of Welfare Economics*, London: Oxford University Press.

Sen, A. K. (1982), *Choice, Welfare and Measurement*, Cambridge Mass.: MIT Press.

On Chapter 7:

Harsanyi, J. C. (1955), 'Cardinal welfare, individualistic ethics and interpersonal comparisons of utility;', *Journal of Political Economy*, **63** (4), August.

Möller, R. (1983), *Interpersonelle Nutzenvergleiche*, Göttingen: Vandenhoeck and Ruprecht.

Robbins, L. (1938), 'Interpersonal comparisons of utility', *Economic Journal*, **48** (4), December

On Chapter 8:

Layard, R. ed. (1976), *Cost-Benefit Analysis. Selected Readings*, Harmondsworth: Penguin.

Mishan, E. J. (1971), *Cost-Benefit-Analysis*, London: Allen and Unwin.

Rhoads, St. E. (1980), *Valuing Life: Public Policy Dilemmas*, Boulder Co.: Westview.

On Chapter 9:

Atkinson, A. B. (1983), *The Economics of Inequality* (2nd ed.), Oxford: Oxford University Press.

Deutsch, M. (1985), *Distributive Justice*, New Haven: Yale University Press.

Meade, J. E. (1976), *The Just Economy*, London: Allen and Unwin.

Sen, A. K. (1973), *On Economic Inequality*, Oxford: Clarendon.

Swenson, P. (1989), *Fair Shares*, Ithaca: Cornell University Press.

Tawney, R. H. (1965), *Equality*, London: Allen and Unwin.

Name Index

Subject Index